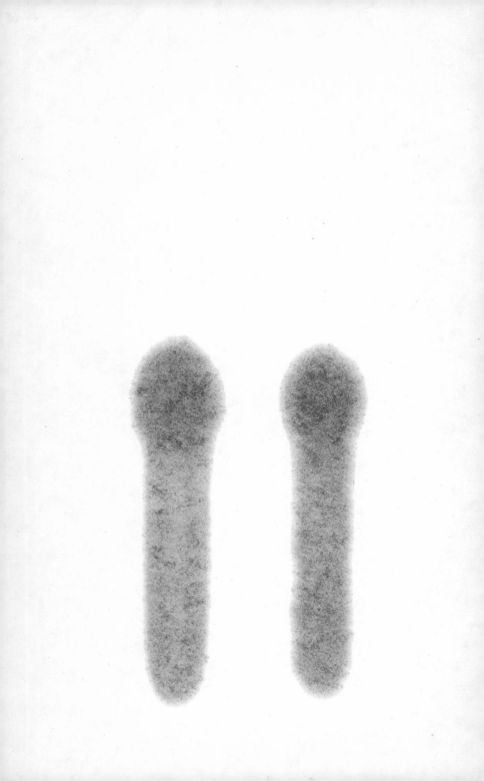

Nobody's Daughter

Aviva Layton
Nobody's Daughter

McClelland and Stewart

The Canadian Publishers
McClelland and Stewart Limited
25 Hollinger Road, Toronto M4B 3G2

Canadian Cataloguing in Publication Data

Layton, Aviva, 1933-
  Nobody's daughter

ISBN 0-7710-4816-5

I. Title.

PS8573.A88N62   C813'.54   C82-094079-8
PR9199.3.L388N62

Printed and bound in Canada

CONTENTS

Part I

A Fistful of Rags

My Aunty Milly had a huge hole in her chest. When I put my fist into it I could feel an obscene throbbing of veins and heart — it was like plunging a hand into a nest of warm freshly slaughtered sparrows. My mother told me that the hole was there because my grandmother had severe bronchitis when she was carrying Aunty Milly and for the last few months of pregnancy she had to sit up bent almost double. It was in this position — hunched over like an old crone — that she was delivered of her fourth daughter. As a result, Aunty Milly had a hollow in her chest which, with advancing puberty, grew deeper and deeper. While her sisters billowed out into milky mounds, Aunty Milly grew inwards, her fragile yellow-white skin stretched taut, the superfluous nipples on either side of the hole purple and wrinkled like old grapes.

She was, needless to say, the family sacrifice. My grand-mother died shortly after Milly was born. Not even leaving the harshness of Russian winters for the heat of Australia could save her from multiple lung infections. She left behind her, stranded in an alien land, a bewildered husband and four daughters. The four daughters represented with almost mathematical precision — and in defiance of all fairy tales — descending degrees of beauty. The eldest, Sonya, was the most gifted — she was artistic and beautiful. The next,

Bashka, was pretty, plump, sweet-natured. Then came Fanya, my mother — lumpish, short-sighted, frizzy-haired, shrewd. A dog. And finally Milly. Squat forehead, lanky dark-brown hair, scrawny-limbed, hollow-chested. One by one the girls married off — Sonya to a sickly, sensitive violin teacher; Bashka to an impoverished but gentle and adoring bookseller; and Fanya to a born bachelor who, twenty years her senior, was passionately unconcerned with "making a living" or "having a family" and wanted only to be left alone. He had strayed unwarily into the house of my grandfather and found out too late that it was a sticky spiderweb with Fanya sitting hungrily in the middle. He was swallowed up, Feivel my father, in one fast greedy gulp.

Milly was, of course, designated as the spinster daughter who was to "look after Papa." She was born to be a maiden aunt. As soon as her sisters gave birth to children, she became Aunty Milly, and that was that. She was never to escape. I learnt quickly to treat her with an undisguised contempt for which I was constantly punished, although it mirrored faithfully the unexpressed contempt which her whole family felt for her.

I felt contempt for my Aunty Milly, but I also loved her because I could manipulate her to satisfy my every whim. She was a never-ending source of ice lollies, india rubber balls and matchbox toys. Especially matchbox toys. I was crazy about them. I must have bullied her into buying me dozens and dozens of these matchbox-shaped containers in which lived whole families of celluloid dollies. My favourite was the one with the little bride and groom. They lay chastely side by side, their heads on tiny pink cushions, covered by a matching lolly-pink quilted "sateen" coverlet. I would carry that box with me everywhere, whipping it out at odd moments of the day and quickly shoving it open, as if to surprise the unsuspecting occupants. What was I hoping to discover? A full-scale copulation with the groom dolly humping away on top of the bride dolly? A tell-tale bloodstain on the coverlet? Not that I was conscious of such matters at the innocent age of six but I *did* feel that if I opened the box quickly enough, one day something — some unnamed mystery — would be revealed to me.

I also possessed — again by bullying Aunty Milly — a whole army of larger naked pink celluloid dolls with perpetually wide-open china-blue eyes, moveable limbs and nothing — not even a hint of a declivity — between the dimpled thighs. Nothing there meant that it was a girl — that much I knew. My chief delight was to dress up these dolls and for that I needed a constant supply of material. My Aunty Milly was the chief supplier of this commodity too. In the hollow of her chest she used to stuff dozens of pieces of coloured rags. Why she didn't use handkerchiefs or old slips or torn pillowcases to stuff that ugly hole, I didn't think to ask her. Certainly they would have fulfilled their function with far more efficiency than the snippets of rags she obtained from some source unknown to anyone except herself.

I don't know when it occurred to me that the stuffing in Aunty Milly's hole would make the perfect wardrobe for my dolls. All I remember is that at frequent intervals — in front of other people, in shops, even in the street — I would unbutton the front of her dress and, in a lightning flash, plunge my hand into that warm foetid hole and emerge with a triumphant fistful of rags. Aunty Milly would howl her outrage, my mother would beat me, my other aunts would give me a "talking to." They would even offer me generous swatches of remnants with which to clothe my dolls. I spurned them. I wanted Aunty Milly's rags. Why? I think it had something to do with odour, warmth and the brutish power I exercised over my subservient aunt. I also suspected she experienced a secret thrill in being able to offer herself — I grabbed, she gave. From that bony sterile cavern came something other than disgust, disappointment, a failed life. . . .

There was only one way in which my Aunty Milly had power over me, her tyrannizer. That was on the nights when my parents, unable to get a baby-sitter, took me to sleep over at her place. We would lie together, my Aunty Milly and I, in her narrow bed, she at one end, me at the other, her dry, horny bunioned feet thrust into my face.

"Tell me a story," I'd say. I would refuse to go to sleep before she did.

"Not tonight," she'd pretend.

"Yes, tonight. Now. Otherwise I'll get up and go home."

We knew we were playing a game. It was a game we both enjoyed except that my enjoyment was mixed with a dread of what I knew was to come. There in the dark Aunty Milly would drop her voice and start chanting. Her disembodied voice, which bore no relationship to the smelly feet against my cheek, floated up from the far end of the bed. Aunty Milly became a Presence, a Voice from Beyond.

"It was a da-ark and stormy night," intoned the sepulchral voice. "And the rain came down in torrents. And Anna said, 'Come, tell me a tale.' And the tale goes on for e-v-e-r. . . . "

No matter how many times I heard this dirge, I was struck with terror, and Aunty Milly knew it. But time and time again I'd ask for it, beg to be frightened, beg my Aunty Milly to turn herself into a ghoul, a ghost, a witch. . . .

Often, at home in my own bed, I'd try to frighten myself. "It was a da-ark and stormy ni-ight. And the rain came down in torrents. . . " I'd drawl. Sometimes it worked quickly; sometimes it took ages for me to feel anything. But I would not abandon the constant repetition of the magic words until I could feel the old familiar sense of terror invade the security of my bed.

———⟨⟩———

When my mother brought me home from the hospital, where she'd given birth both to me and the hemorrhoids which were to plague her for the rest of her life, I cried all through the first night and didn't stop crying for the next thirty months. I shrieked and sobbed and yowled my way through the first two and a half years of my life. When I finally slept through three consecutive hours, my distraught mother was convinced I had died and prodded me awake to reassure herself that I was still alive.

I know that it's supposed to be impossible for me to remember those nights of incessant howling — but I do. Even now, I can conjure up my misery, my sense of abandonment. There was nothing to comfort me in the bleak world into which I had been born. I spat out the proffered nipple. No nourishment there. What I wanted was to be fed, held, caressed, rocked into comfort; what I received were abrupt nasty jolts of anxiety. I kicked against my mother's arms. I fought against the treachery of sleep.

In despair, Fanya consulted specialists. "Give her brandy." "Give her sugared water." "Swaddle her." "Rub her with warm oil."

Finally, the solution. As soon as I started to howl, my mother was to uncover me and put me outside on the verandah. I was to be kept cold and smelly and hungry for hours. Then I was to be brought inside, fed and warmed. If I so much as whimpered I was to be whisked back out on the verandah. "Do this every night for one month!" pronounced Dr. Mandel. "And if you still have a problem, come back to me."

It worked like the charm it was. I learnt fast and the lesson stayed, the foundation of a life-long style. The formula was simple — if you want to be warm and happy and secure, first you have to be cold and unhappy and insecure. Feeling good/feeling bad — like love and marriage, they went together like a horse and carriage. Trouble is, even to this day I'm slightly confused. I can't remember what is supposed to come first — does coldness guarantee warmth? Or is it the other way around?

13

Fat, Black Zero

Scene: There is white mosquito netting around my cot. I am lying half asleep. It is twilight. Dreamily I pick my nose. Soft. Mushy. Delicious. Suddenly a nosebleed. I stand up in my cot and wipe my nose on the netting. Great splotches of mucousy red on the white of the net. I stare, wipe my nose again, stare. I try to cover as much of the net as I can with the lovely colours which I've been clever enough to manufacture all by myself. . . . I feel proud and lie back in bed to contemplate my exquisite handiwork.

I hear my mother tiptoeing into my room. She'll be pleased to see what I've done. Instead, she shrieks, "Look at the mess! Oi, what a filthy mess! Look what she's done. She hasn't killed me enough already, she has to do this to me! Out of spite she does it. Pure spite! I don't work hard enough like a dog? She has to do this to me to top off a day. . . . Even a dog is entitled to a little peace. . . . "

I feel angry, frightened, guilty. My heart is beating wildly.

Scene: The bathroom sink is blocked up. My mother allows me to brush my teeth over the bath. I spit out a jet of saliva and toothpaste. It sprays against the enamel of the bath.

White on white. A mote of sunlight catches it and I feel a shooting surge of joy. I stare, entranced by the creamy delicate tracery. The moment hangs suspended in the syrupy sunbeam. Then my mother bursts through the door. With an abrupt gesture she turns on the tap, exclaiming about the time I take to do a simple thing like brushing my teeth. She goes on and on. The fine web of white is completely obliterated under the rush of tap water. So is my moment of pure joy.

Somewhere deep inside me a hard little acorn of hate is growing. . . .

Scene: It is my fourth birthday. I am being forced to share it with the child of my parents' best friends who live next door. His name is Carlton. He is two months older than I and he's fat and pudgy and white. I despise him. Our parents are "bringing us up together." We sit in high chairs at either end of the long mahogany dining table. On our heads are paper crowns — Carlton is King and I am Queen. All the way down the table, places are set with paper crackers, bowls of raspberry jelly, little cardboard baskets full of multi-coloured boiled lollies. I sit, seemingly quiet and calm, under my silvered crown waiting for the guests to arrive. But I'm not quiet and calm. I'm seething with anxiety. No one will bring two presents; they will forget that there are two birthdays. They'll bring one thing for both of us and it will be a Carlton thing.

Why can't I have my *own* birthday? If I'm a queen, why does there have to be a king? I like his crown better than mine. It's gold. I don't despise Carlton anymore. I hate and fear him.

Soon after that, I began to taunt Carlton. "Cauliflower!" I'd yell at him. "Cauliflower Carlton!" I would chase him out of his front yard and down the street shrieking after him so that the whole neighbourhood could hear. "Cauliflower. Cauliflower," I'd shriek like a wild banshee, until he burst into tears and ran home.

I was given a thrashing by my mother but it didn't daunt me one bit. I felt proud and satisfied. I was the stronger of the two. I had finally proved it. I'd reduced him to tears. The booby. The weak snivelling fat booby. . . .

Scene: What a clever little neurotic I am! How inventive! I have managed with much cunning and ingenuity to turn a source of undiluted pleasure — thumb-sucking — into a source of acute anxiety. With my left thumb in my mouth and my index finger stroking gently along one side of my nose, I am able to convince myself that I am invulnerable, impervious to all outside attacks. Now I — or some vicious demon — has managed to ruin my peace of mind. I cannot enjoy the tranquility my thumb-sucking confers upon me unless my left forearm is icy cold. And I mean *icy cold.* My obsession is a stroke of pure masochistic genius, as there is no way of keeping any part of one's flesh cold through the heat of an Australian summer night. I now have to carry to bed with me, surreptitiously, a supply of ice chipped from the ice tray of our wooden icebox, and pack my arm in it until it is numb with cold. Ah, the bliss! My hot thumb in my mouth, my right hand stroking the delicious iciness of my forearm, I drift off into an easy sleep only to wake up hours later with a sickening jolt of disappointment. My forearm has reverted to blood temperature. Another secret trek to the icebox (Fanya would murder me if she knew what a mess I was making!), this time through the silent, sleeping house;

16

and again the cycle repeats itself — the ecstasy of cold, the stealing up of treacherous warmth. And so on all through the hot, sticky night. . . .

—⟨—

My father. He called me the Little Snake. My mother he called the Big Snake. Never had I heard my father call my mother by her name. Never had I heard my father call *me* by my name. Did he even remember what it was? If names had magic — and they had — he was withholding our magic from us. How did he get away with it? He lived in the same house as us and yet he managed, by what eccentric skills I never knew, to avoid ever having to call us into being.

My father couldn't make a living. He insisted on messing up every venture he undertook. It was his way of getting even with my mother for marrying him, for being so unattractive, for bullying him into the respectability for which he was so clearly unsuited.

When she first met him, my father was a barrowman. It was work he loved and was good at. With two others — non-Jews, the *zwei shigotsim*, my mother called them — he was the proprietor of a street barrow selling fruit and vegetables. Their spot was outside a busy downtown arcade; and because their goods were always fresh and they cheerfully threw in a few extra pieces, they developed a thriving business. Every week at the end of their Saturday trading, they would spread out their worn leather aprons and divide the week's take into three parts. "One for you. One for you. One for you." Then they'd pocket their money without even bothering to count it, fill up huge bags of fruit and vegetables for their families, and head home.

My father loved it. On quiet days he would pull a book out of his back pocket and read. Sometimes he even read while he was serving his customers. Although he was no doubt cheated of a few bob, it didn't matter to him and it didn't matter to his partners. There was more than enough to go around.

But not for my mother. She couldn't stand the thought of my father being a barrowman. She nagged and she pleaded until out of sheer weariness — and also out of a deep indifference to the tiresome details of life — my father threw in his leather apron and went, like all respectable Jews, into the *shmatta* trade.

For her pains my mother got nothing, neither status nor money. What she did get was a *nebish* for a husband.

While her friends' husbands made fortunes out of the wartime black market, Feivel maintained a stubborn and pigheaded honesty.

"You'd have to be a fool, a *nar*, not to do good these days," Fanya would storm at my blank-faced father.

Poor Fanya! She had to sit on the sidelines and watch her friends, who had started off much poorer than herself, grow rich. Two-storey mansions, fancy clothes, private Anglican schools for their offspring — all this was possible for them through the hard-working cunning of their husbands. Fanya's husband, on the other hand, had "principles" — my mother said the word with such venom it was years before I discovered it wasn't a swear word.

I think I began to realize even then, with a new respect for my father, that it wasn't only honesty which impelled him — it was revenge. The perfect revenge against which my mother was helpless.

Scene: I'm at school. It's wartime and the teacher is, seemingly for the hundredth time, going around the class asking children what their daddies are doing in the war. Everybody's daddy is "at the front," "in intelligence," "being shipped overseas" or "missing in action"—that's the best thing of all. My daddy's "in business" — and even that's a lie. A more accurate description would be "out of business." I can feel the scorn being heaped on my Jewish head. Only Lotte Ziegler's father is held in more contempt than mine — he's an enemy alien. No matter that he's also Jewish, a refugee from Hitler's Germany. He's officially an "enemy alien." Luckily for me, though, I have an ace up my sleeve. Or an almost-ace. My Uncle Jack, the one married to my sweet-faced Aunty Bashka, is "in munitions." He works in an ammunition factory outside Sydney and although he's in no imminent danger of being shot, drowned, torpedoed, beheaded — he's still helping, he's doing something for the war effort. Even more important, he's helping me (not that he knows it) get through my school days without feeling like a traitor to my country.

Why wasn't Uncle Jack my father? Why wasn't Aunty Bashka my mother? I spent much of my childhood asking myself these questions and I always came up with the wrong answers. I wished with all my heart that I lived with them. They didn't have any children of their own, although Uncle Jack often talked of having "a couple of little nippers" as soon as they could afford them. Privately I used to wonder why they just didn't forget about the "little nippers" and settle for me instead. The times I got to stay over at their place were special. I slept on the living-room sofa. In the morning the sun spilt in through the windows and Uncle Jack sang out in his impeccable English accent (he was that exotic creature, an English Jew), "Rise and shine! Rise and shine!"

Why didn't *I* have a father who called out "Rise and shine!" each morning? A father who knew what to do with nuts and bolts and motors. Instead, what did I have? A *nar*, a *gornisht*, and worse — a scholar, a bookworm. A father who, as soon as he read a book that he admired, went out and bought a dozen copies and gave them away to his rich cronies. And his English was despicable! When we walked together down the street, I tried to lag behind in case I met someone I knew. I dreaded the ridicule of having a "reffo" for a father, of being called a "bloody Yid." When my mother was too busy and he had to write a note to my teacher, he started off with "Greetings! Hello, Teacher." He couldn't write, as all fathers did, "Dear Miss Herlihy," comma. Next line. Indent. "Please excuse my daughter Anna's absence from school on Thursday, 18th February inst."

No, he couldn't write "my daughter Anna" because he even refused to *say* it, so how could he be expected to send a proper note to a creature called Miss Herlihy who ate ham sandwiches on white bread which had the crusts trimmed off (I saw them once with my own eyes) and wore blue glass beads threaded on a piece of black velvet around her scrawny Gentile neck; Miss Herlihy whose thin lips drew back in a snarl over her dry dentures when she read such a Jewy note.

No. I had to have a father who instead of buying me Felix the Cat comic books handed me cheaply printed pamphlets titled "Natasha, Girl Parachutist" or "Vladimir Ilyich Lenin, Little Father." No wonder I spent my entire childhood thinking that all Russians were Jews and that "Kalinka Maya" was the Jewish national anthem. Once for a birthday present — I was desperately hoping for a puppy — he presented me with a book called *They All Were Jews*. It contained fascinating and little-known facts — that Jews had invented the wheel, the airplane, the Spinning Jenny ("I should care what your anti-Semite of a teacher tells you? Think for yourself, dummy. Jenny's a Jewish name, no?") It said that Jews had discovered America, electricity, radium, the Northwest Passage; a Jew was the first to walk over Niagara on a tightrope — he'd changed his name from Blumenthal to Blondin because the French were such anti-Semites; and that Jewish blood ran through the veins of all European royalty.

And why didn't I have a father who bought me bobbies

and curls at the lolly shop, and gave me piggybacks when he came home after a hard day's work at the office?

Why, instead, did I have to have a father who . . . fucked me?

Or tried to. True, he didn't go all the way, but the fact remains that sweet scholarly Feivel tried to stick his cock up his little daughter's seven-year-old cunt.

Scene: Sunday morning. A hot, heavy Sunday. I get up and pad over to my parents' bedroom. I want to lie in bed with them, to burrow into that comforting soupy warmth. But I already know deep down, don't I, that coziness and comfort are not to be found with my mother and father, that mine is not a "normal" household and that — most frightening of all — I'm not a "normal" child. So it's a mystery to me why I want to share their bed.

I crawl into one side of the bed. My mother is on the other side . . . sleeping? My father is in the middle. I turn my back to him and close my eyes. A few tense minutes pass. Sun slashes the bed. Crickets thrum insanely. Next door, some children are slogging a ball against a fence. Soon I'll join them. But first. . .

My father undoes the cord of his striped cotton pajama bottoms. He lifts up the hem of my little sky-blue Broderie Anglaise nightie. Very tenderly. Very delicately. Perhaps it's the most delicate gesture he's made in his entire life. He slips his cock between my legs. Against my slit. And moves. A quiet stealthy rhythmical movement that shakes the bed and makes it creak. What, then, is happening to my mother, she who wakes up at the "drop of a pin"? Something awful is happening only inches away from her and she's *sleeping*? Why doesn't she wake up and scream? Or laugh? Or attack her husband? Or rescue her abused and abusing daughter? Who is not screaming. Who is not sleeping. Who, although she feels a hot and secret shame, is enjoying it. She lets her father push and thrust against her until he gives a grunt and something warm and sticky wets her thighs. Then he turns away from her without a word and she gets up out of bed, takes off her soiled and creased nightdress, dresses herself in the crisp clean sundress her nanny has laid out for her the night before, and skips outside to play.

—◆—

Every Sunday morning for nearly one year, I went back to that bed. I had become the seducer, my father the passive recipient. I wasn't content with just Sundays. Sometimes my mother would go out for the evening, leaving me in my father's care. I'd already be in bed tucked into my coverlet, the one which was patterned with scenes from "The Three Pigs." A pretty little girl in a pretty little bed. "Daddy, bring me a glass of water," I'd chirp. He'd ignore me. Again. "Daddy, Daddy. . . " Was he tussling with his conscience in the living room, a biography of Spinoza in his trembling hands? Or was he just ignoring me as usual? "Daddy, I want a glass of water." I was sick of the game now. I wanted to go to sleep, to forget about whatever it was I needed. But something else took over. "A drink of water!" I'd yell.

My father would appear in the darkened doorway. There would be no glass of water in his hands. He would approach my bed.

Eagerly?
Reluctantly?
Brazenly?
Stealthily?
Guiltily?
Did he unbutton his fly?
Did I pull up my nightie?

Did I unbutton his fly?

Did he pull up my nightie?

I don't remember. What I do remember was that comforting, disturbing cock between my little girl's thighs.

And my hating it.

My loving it.

———✧———

Every Saturday afternoon Carlton took me to the pictures. It didn't matter what was playing — we went because it was Saturday. The main feature was always boring. It was the serials we came for. Our parents dressed us up and made Carlton call for me, even though we lived next door to each other. That was something they found cute.

One Saturday *The Lodger* was playing. I was riveted. The lodger killed his victims in such a way that he left his brand on them — everyone knew that it was the lodger who had struck. Their eyes were rolled back into their heads with terror; their mouths opened in a silent agonized scream; their hands were clapped over their ears. Victim after victim. They'd always be found dead at night so that in order to discover the murders, the police officer would have to flash a beam of light over them. The beam would poke and jab around the porch or the living room or the alleyway.

My heart froze in anticipation. Suddenly, a thunder clap of music and the beam would find its target — the eyes gleaming whitely, the mouth wet and drooling, the hands frozen to the side of the head.

After that, I had so many nightmares that my matinee dates were stopped. I was glad. I never wanted to be in such a vulnerable position again — a sitting-duck for whatever nightmare images the theatre manager decided to project onto his screen. . . .

I don't remember when I started doing it to myself.

Months, years later? I would jump in front of a mirror in a dimly lit room, my eyes distorted, my jaw slack, my hands clapped in agonized paralysis to the sides of my head. Terrifying myself. . . .

———✦———

I never wanted to be called Anna Cohen. What I longed for more than anything was to be called Gloria — the name that went with corkscrew curls and starched pinnies and calm controlled mothers, and fathers who didn't try to do things to their little daughters. My last name was a problem too. I couldn't give myself an Irish name or a Scottish one. So I turned my last name, Cohen, back to front. Gloria Nehoc. I scrawled it inside all my books. Wrote it on the inside of my schoolbag. Whispered it to myself before I went to sleep at night. Gloria Nehoc — now *there* was a name!

———✦———

Scene: "Good night, Nanny."
　"Good night."
　"Good night, Nanny."
　"Good night."
　"Good night, Nanny."
　"Good night."
It is my nanny's night out. A weekly occurrence. A weekly tragedy. She is disappearing down the lane leading away from our house and I can feel the cord between us getting thinner and thinner. I have to yell out and hear her reply for as long as the connection can remain. As soon as her voice trails away and dies, I feel totally lost. There is only my father and my mother left. I want my nanny back. I howl out my misery to the house.

"There she goes again," snaps my mother. "Crying over a
proste Australian *shiksa*. Irish-Australian too, into the bargain.
One of these days I'll have to let that girl go."

I'm meant to hear that. It's the only thing that will make
me quieten down my forlorn wails.

——◆——

That girl, that Australian *shiksa*, was who I wished my mother
would be. Nanny. Thelma. My mother had hired her to look
after me when I had whooping cough, and after that she just
stayed on. Although she was barely twenty, she had white
porcelain squares in her mouth attached to lolly-pink gleaming strips — these were supposed to resemble teeth and gums.
Her hair was a carroty frizz, and her white skin was blotched
with freckles.

A real *proste shiksa*, if ever there was one, but I loved her.
She was the only one I could rely on in my topsy-turvy life.
When she took her one night of the week off to meet
whatever vile and hated rival she kept company with, I felt
the bottom drop out of my world. I was terrified she wouldn't
come back, that she'd leave me in the care of a mother I dis-
liked and distrusted.

Each morning after her night out I woke up trembling
and full of a terrible foreboding. Had she abandoned me to
my parents? I raced into her back bedroom. What relief —
she was there. I jumped into her bed — *her* warmth I loved —
and we rolled around in the sheets and kissed and cuddled
and laughed.

——◆——

Scene: It's Christmastime and Aunty Milly has taken me to
see Santa Claus at one of the big department stores. This

year they have put him at the top of a tall chimney. One of Santa's helpers herds groups of excited children into a small recess and instructs them to look up the chimney where they'll see Santa swing himself down, a huge sack of toys slung over his shoulder.

I'm at the edge of one of the groups. In front of me I hear exclamations of delight as one by one each child looks up to see the magical sight. Finally it's my turn. My heart is beating with excitement. I stare up into the murky heights of the chimney. Nothing. Nothing except a big fat black zero. It's too late. Santa has left for the day.

"Come again tomorrow," says Santa's helper.

But there *is* no tomorrow, I want to yell out in my sorrow and disappointment. There is only now and I've missed out. Santa Claus will visit every child except me. Goy that he is, Fanya wouldn't let him in, even if he pounded on the door.

I'm left out again, just like the little ragged beggar-maid who stands out in the cold snow, her nose pressed against the brightly lit pane, looking in at the roaring log-fire, the decorated Yule tree, the happy family tying baubles on the branches or wrapping gifts in bright paper. Staring at the table loaded with goodies for everyone except her. . . .

The Rise and Fall
of the Trouser Princess

"Crikey!" screams my furious Uncle Misha in his heavy Russian-Yiddish accent. "Strike me pink! It's crook, it's crook — you're playing crook!"

These unlikely expressions — Misha thinks he's speaking a perfect English — strike terror into my eight-year-old heart.

"Strike me pink!" he shouts again and jabs my violin under my chin with such force I feel as if it's going to come out the back of my neck.

Twice a week Uncle Misha, Sonya's husband, gave me violin lessons. I dreaded them. I dreaded the sudden volcanic bursts of rage which Uncle Misha unleashed at unexpected intervals. I dreaded Palings, the decrepit old building where he had his studio. Any music teacher who was anybody at all in Sydney had a studio in Palings, but why anybody would actually *want* to be there was a mystery to me. It was a nightmare of a place. When I stepped out of the bright sunshine, I felt I'd entered some gloomy cave.

If I was too early or Uncle Misha was still busy with a pupil, I had to wait at his padded dark-green door. Outside other doors stood similar figures, most of them, like myself, clutching black coffin-like cases. Since I had just finished reading my first Dracula story, I imagined that the cases were brimming with Transylvanian soil into which we, Dracula's victims, would sink as soon as we passed through those padded doors.

That thought terrified me, but what terrified me more was the hideous old lift. It was operated by pulling on a length of greasy rope which ran through a hole in its floor. The rope-puller of this awful contraption was an ancient World War I veteran called Ernie. Instead of forearms and hands, Ernie had two leather devices with hooks coming out from each end. By maneuvering his hooks around the rope and leaning forward on it, Ernie was able to make the lift rise at the rate of an inch a minute. Each time he did it, his face would contort in pain.

I lived in mortal dread that one day, through some gruesome error on his part, Ernie was going to catch his hooks into the frayed parts of the rope and break it clean in two. Then we'd plunge to our doom, old Ernie and me, into the murky depths below. And as if that weren't enough, every time I entered the lift — the stairwell was so dim and spooky I didn't even consider it — Ernie would start in on his little game. "Let old Ern 'ave a go on yer fiddle, bub. I bet I can fiddle real good, eh, mate? Be a sport, let's 'ave a go!" He'd lunge forward and claw at my violin case with his metal hook while I, terrified out of my wits, shrank back against the walls of the lift.

The only thing which kept me coming back to Palings week after week was the special attention it got me in the family. My violin playing seemed to be the only thing which Fanya was proud of; it even moved Feivel to a mumbled word of praise. But it was Sonya whose opinion really mattered. "She's a highly gifted little violinist," she'd tell my admiring family. "A second Heifetz. A little Menuhin."

And Aunty Sonya should have known what she was talking about. As well as being the beauty of the family, she was also recognized as the artistic one, the "artiste." Whatever goodies were going around, she got them — the piano lessons, the boat trip to Palestine with her mother. One of my favourite family stories was of the young handsome English lord who met my Aunty Sonya on board ship and fell madly in love with her. As he wasn't allowed to invite her to the first-class section where he had his suite, he spent all his time in the tourist section trying to persuade Sonya to marry him. That was the part of the story I especially loved. The part I didn't like was where she turned him down. One of the reasons was because he wasn't Jewish (even though he swore he'd "turn") but mostly it was because he was not an "artiste" like my aunt, and so was not worthy of her love. "He might be a lord," Sonya had said, "but he can't buy my heart with a title."

Although I liked the ring of these words, I liked the ring of "Lady Sonya" even more and bitterly regretted that she hadn't changed her mind. I was always hoping that if I heard the story often enough, the ending would turn out differently.

The man who ended up winning the hand of the beauteous Sonya was Misha Stavrosky. Uncle Misha, a poor sickly stick of a man who could hardly speak English, was only a violin teacher, it was true, but he was "highly gifted," a "true artist," and, as such, won the heart of my Aunty Sonya.

After they were married, Sonya took charge of his career. She rented a cheap room in the suburbs for Misha's studio and advertised in the local paper for pupils. Soon Misha's reputation had spread to such a degree that he was able to get a studio at Palings, and students begged for a chance to be put on his waiting list. At this point, Sonya's airs and graces became so pronounced — or so her sisters thought — that they could barely tolerate her. But I was her darling, the gifted child it seemed she was destined not to have. Convinced that I was born to be a great violinist, she took charge of my "musical education." Fanya gave in and handed me over. ("Poor Sonya. She'll never have any children of her own. One look at that *loksh* she calls a husband and you can see why. A fiddle he might know about, but believe you me, that's it!")

Every afternoon Sonya arrived at our house to supervise

my practice, clouds of Evening in Paris billowing about her. And at her twice-yearly "musicales" I was the star, my nimble little bow flying over the strings in a Vivaldi concerto or a Boccherini minuet, the hushed devotion of the audience almost making up for the terrors of Misha's unpredictable temper or the Palings' lift.

Then one day Ernie made a lunge not for my violin case but for me, and pinning me up against the lift wall, he pulled my skirt up with one hook and my pants down with the other.

That was the excuse I had been waiting for. I jerked myself free, raced out of the building and returned home. Luckily no one was there. I dumped my violin, my bow with the special markings and my whole supply of resins into the garbage can. I clanged down the lid and sat on top of it, my arms folded, to await the return of my parents.

In vain my family implored me not to turn my back on what Sonya wailed was my God-given gift. But neither her desperate pleadings nor Uncle Misha's "Strike me pink!" could change my mind. I simply stood there and let the storm rage over my head. Anna had bowed out. Let Jascha and Yehudi reign supreme.

My grandfather — Grandfather Zuckerman — ran a small dingy tailor shop in a run-down section of Sydney. "The Trouser King" he called himself, and he had a huge sign outside his shop to back up his claim. Me, he called "The Trouser Princess," and for years I really believed that I was royalty. Somehow or another, the royal blood had skipped a generation, leaving my mother and her sisters out of it altogether.

As a Trouser Princess, I was granted many privileges. My favourite one was being able to look at my grandfather's gold fob watch which he wore in his waistcoat pocket. "It is a special watch," he'd say in his thick Yiddish accent. "It wears out by looking at it. Only to Trouser Princesses do I show it, but even then, only for a second or two."

Despite his high title, my grandfather was a very bad tailor. Worse, he simply wasn't a tailor at all. The slacks he used to make me out of thick dark itchy remnants would always have one leg shorter than the other, the clumsily sewn crotch biting its way into my cleft until I felt I was being sawn in half.

The wonder was that my grandfather's shop flourished. No Jew would be seen dead near the place. Only *shigotsim* flocked to the shop. "Id-yots" my grandfather called them, spitting out the last syllable as if it were a piece of undigested food. And id-yots they must have been to tolerate my grandfather's insults and curses.

My mother often dropped me off at the store when she went shopping, and I'd cringe with shame in the cutting room when I heard a customer come into the shop for a fitting. My grandfather, tape measure hanging around his neck like a professional, would trot out some dusty old bolt of material and drape it around the poor victim.

It was in vain for the customer to protest that it wasn't even the colour he'd chosen, let alone the material. "Brown you want? Id-yot!" bellowed my grandfather. His voice rang with a fierce conviction. "Brown! With your colouring, your complexion! You want you should look like a mud pie? Like a lump of *sheis*?"

Shaking, I would cower under the wooden table, waiting for the customer to crack my grandfather's jaw open with one heave of his tough, goy fist. But always there would be a subservient silence. When I got up enough courage to peek around the corner, there would be a huge, shambling hulk, head hanging, feet shuffling, hands twisted in front of him, while my grandfather's insults rained down upon his head.

Like lions the customers walked in. Like castrated sheep

31

they shuffled out, holding under their arms a clumsy brown paper package containing some butchered lump of material for which they had handed over a goodly part of their hard-earned pay. Or they would walk out with the suit on, hopping from leg to leg, distorting their bodies to make up for the discrepancy in the arm length, the tightness across the left shoulder, the crookedness of the seams which were already beginning to split open.

"Mr. Zuckerman," they would dare to say, already cowed from two previous fittings, "wouldn't you say there's a little shortness in one arm?" And the poor chump would apologetically extend one raw wrist which protruded a good four inches from an ill-made cuff.

"Id-yot!" my grandfather would shout. "Pull it down! Pull it! Can I help it if you stood like a crippled crab at the last fitting? What do you want from me — my life? That I should spit blood because you want to impress your girl friend?" (Not for nothing was he Fanya's father.) "You want you should come in here with your *pishach* money and expect from me Savile Row? A frog you came in! A prince you walk out! And already you know only complaints! Leave already. Go! And next time you should want a suit, don't come to The Trouser King. Go rather to the pub and drink your money away like the rest of your *farshtunkine* tribe!"

Why didn't the customer whip out a pistol from his overcoat pocket and shoot my grandfather between the eyes? "Bang, bang! Take that, you filthy Yid!" Or why didn't he grab my grandfather's arm and twist it right out of its socket? Cr-a-ack! No. Instead, he stammered and apologized and shuffled out of the door sideways. And sure enough, when next he wanted a suit he'd be back at The Trouser King, his head bowed to receive his ill-fitted jacket and his portion of insults.

What spell, I wondered, did my grandfather, The Trouser King, cast over his servile population? My belief in his royalty deepened. He was a king and I his princess. Then a terrible thing happened. My grandfather's brother Benny opened a tailor shop less than two blocks from his brother's emporium. He called it "The Trouser King." It was just as in the fairy tales — the true king was the victim of his wicked brother's usurpation. But unlike the fairy tales, my grandfather didn't take sword in hand and do battle for his kingdom. Instead, he had another sign erected which read "The Original Trouser King." My belief began to wobble.

It shattered finally a year or two later when I was old enough to go around town by myself. I found that Sydney was infested with royalty. The Tie King, The Button King, The Umbrella King. My faith bit the dust. It was heart-breakingly clear to me that if my grandfather was not The Trouser King, then I was not The Trouser Princess. From that moment on, my grandfather ceased to hold much interest for me. And when, sensing this, he'd dangle his gold watch in front of me so that I could look at it as much as I wanted, I turned my face away in indifference.

Scene: I'm staring into the mirror. It's late at night. My mother and father are asleep. I've woken out of a nightmare in which everything, including myself, is blank, a total nothingness. I lie in bed, soaked in sweat, my heart galloping, trying to reassure myself of my own existence, of the existence of the world. I pinch myself, pull my fingers, tap my teeth, bang my head on the pillow. I want the pressure of solidity, of one object encountering another and showing evidence of the encounter, even if it means pain.

Nothing helps. I get out of bed. The floor is made of chewing gum — it sags and sways beneath me. I fall against a wall. It gives. I'm in a grey, raggy chewing-gum world where nothing holds to its own contours, where everything dissolves.

If I look into a mirror, will anything be there? Will I still

have a pair of eyes fixed into my skull? I find a mirror and
stare into it. I see my face, I see my eyes, but I can't see
myself. I push my face up against the mirror. My eyelashes
are batting up against the mirror-image eyelashes. I look
straight into my own eyes and they dissolve into a grey milky
gumminess. I feel as if I'm disappearing into my own jelly.

I kiss myself on the lips; try to push my tongue into my
mouth. The mirror finally gives me the reassurance I so
desperately want. It is cold, hard, unyielding. It holds. I
keep my mouth jammed up tight to the mirror. Saliva dribbles
down my chin, down the mirror.

My mother used to take me to the Royal Easter Show which
was held every Easter at the showground right around the
corner from our house. I adored it. It was the highlight of
my life, not the least because I saw my mother actually
enjoying herself. Amazingly enough, we both loved the
same things and they had nothing to do with the live-
stock, farm machinery and agricultural produce. First,
we'd head for the decorated cake section of the Country
Women's Association, where the only rule seemed to be that
a cake be made to look as unlike a cake as human ingenuity
could manage. There were cakes that looked like radios, like
gas stoves, like midget cellos (with accompanying musical
scores in pink and silver frosted icing); cakes like antique
automobiles, like koala bears.

What happened to them, I wondered, when the show was
over? Did the Country Women's children eat them? Or did
they just go mouldy and have to be thrown onto the dust
heap? The whole thing fascinated me and if I didn't know
the sideshows were waiting, I would have lingered there the
whole day.

But the real reason for coming to the show was to see the

freaks. There were dozens of them. They came back year after year like old friends, and I believed in all of them. The Snow Queen who lived in the heart of a block of ice; the fat lady dressed in a bright-red tutu; the African boy with the curly pig's tail. One of my favourites was the hermaphrodite who dressed like a medieval jester in motley — one-half was an extravagantly coutured woman with a Joan Crawford suit, shiny black shoes (or rather, shoe), a cocktail hat with a black velvet spotted veil. The other half was a smart gentleman in a pin-striped suit, fedora hat, tan Oxford shoe. No detail was neglected — one hand was delicately manicured; the other was coarse and heavy, with hair sprouting from the knuckles. The face was halved too — lipstick, mascara, eye shadow and rouge on one side; a long curly black beard on the other. I could have stared for hours at the Man-Lady. And my mother, who for some weird reason was relaxed, permissive and even contented, allowed me as much time as I wanted.

One year there was a new attraction — the Pinheaded Chinaman. I was resentful that a new freak had intruded on familiar territory but I was still eager to see him. Inside the tent was a small rectangle filled with sawdust presided over by a man dressed as a ringmaster in top hat, shabby gold-braided uniform and long whip. He held a yellow wizened Chinese man by the hand. He was almost exactly my height, but he looked centuries old. On his shoulders sat a tiny fragile bobbing head — a pinhead, just as the posters promised — with beady black-button slitted eyes. They looked as if they'd been daubed onto his parchment face by a clumsy hand.

The audience stood behind the ropes while the ringmaster led the Pinheaded Chinaman around to shake hands with everyone. Before taking their hands, he made a ceremonious bow in front of each person.

He entranced me. I adored him. I made up my mind to take him home and I had visions of getting a big enough matchbox and popping him in and out whenever the fancy took me. Dancing with impatience, I could barely wait until he made his way around the ropes to where I stood. But a horrible thing happened — he ignored my outstretched hand and took my mother's instead. Then he moved on to the next person. I was stricken with grief.

Something at the back of my mind told me what I felt I had always known — that one day I was going to be passed over by a pinheaded Chinaman. The confirmation of this knowledge was overwhelming. I howled. Sensing that this was bad for business, the ringmaster gently tugged the Chinaman back in my direction. Again he ignored me and tried to move on. People started to titter. I howled more insistently. Taking the Chinaman by the hand, the ringmaster pushed him towards me. His eyes, which were on a level with mine, shot me a look of malevolence and, chattering in some sort of high-pitched gibberish, he sprang back into the centre of the arena.

Scalding tears poured down my face and Fanya tried to persuade me to leave. But nothing would budge me. He *had* to shake hands with me, *had* to acknowledge the bond I knew there was between us. The ringmaster was becoming angrier and angrier. He grabbed the Chinaman's hand and dragged him back to where I was standing. Now the Chinaman was also shrieking, dodging and dancing away from me. There was terror in his eyes. At this point I didn't even care if he gave his formal little bow. My only demand was that he touch me, making some sort of physical contact.

Suddenly the Chinaman ducked his head and viciously bit one of my fingers. Blood started to ooze out. The tittering of the audience stopped abruptly, and some of them started to file out. I was beside myself with pain and outrage at the injustice of it all. For a few moments the Chinaman and I were united in a kinship of howling and misery. Then Fanya dragged me off. I was furiously, hatefully jealous of her because he had shaken hands with her. How dare he? How dare she?

Fanya, in a gesture of unusual sympathy, bought me the most expensive kewpie doll there was. I'd never had one as elaborate as this. This was a Queen kewpie. She dangled from a piece of elastic attached to a wand, and she was dressed in spangles and net and had silver glitter and feathers stuck all over her body. I looked at her covetously for a moment and then threw her on the grass and jumped on her pink celluloid body.

Again and again and again I ground my heels into her until she was cracked through and through and her spangles lay smudged in the dirt. . . .

The Dance of the Caterpillar

My grandfather's mother — my great-grandmother — was over one hundred years old and had only one eye but that eye was enough to strike terror into whomever its glare was directed upon. Everybody, including my grandfather, was terrified of her and she knew it. The only one who didn't stand in awe of her was Aunty Milly. She and I were privy to an awful intimate knowledge about my great-grandmother.

Every Friday afternoon my aunt took care of me, my mother being busy with preparations for the weekend, and I accompanied her on her round. First we would do Bubba's shopping — one dozen oranges, two pickled herrings, one onion, one chalah. Then, laden down with the Sabbath Queen's offerings, we would ascend the steps of the dilapidated Woollahra terrace house to my great-grandmother's room. To me that room seemed like a chamber of horrors. Bubba sat at a small dusty window looking out into a treeless backyard. There was an overpowering stench in the room — it had the sickly-sweet smell of a butcher shop but with the pervasive cloying overtones which only human putrefaction can give off. I knew only too well where it was coming from. Hidden from sight under her dusty dark-blue serge skirt trailed a pink length of intestine. It glistened, pulsated, throbbed, attached by some mysterious lifeline to Bubba's withered arsehole.

38

Whenever we entered, she would turn her one malevolent eye on us as if we were, my aunt and I, personally responsible for the plight in which she found herself — a fierce, proud matriarch, daughter of scholars and rabbis, reduced to a rheumy one-eyed old woman with a prolapsed rectum.

Slowly, painfully, she would rise from her chair and hobble over to the creaking iron bedstead in the corner. There she would lie herself down on her left side, her remaining eye closed in martyred resignation. My aunt would raise her skirt, her numerous yellowing linen petticoats, and as I stood in one corner of the room unable to avert my eyes, I could see Aunty Milly's arm gradually disappearing up my great-grandmother's rectum and hear the soft plish-plash-plop of her intestines being shoved back into place.

Was I revolted by this weekly occurrence? Traumatized? Fascinated? I don't know. I simply went to Bubba's every Friday afternoon, and what happened there was part of our family's ritual. Because my Aunty Milly had a hole in her chest, it seemed right that she was the one chosen to stuff her grandmother's intestines back up into *her* hole.

A hole could be disguised, stuffed, padded — but it always remained for you to fall back into, time and time and time again. . . .

There was a girl on the street named Phyllis. She was a *shiksa*. I hardly ever used that word because I hated it, but it's what Phyllis was and that's all there was to it. She had knobby knees, scaly elbows and curls which were mean and skinny — not at all like the soft springy sausages of Shirley Temple which they were meant to resemble.

Every Saturday morning Phyllis appeared with bandages wrapped around what looked like the sawn-off stumps of her hair. "*Goyim*," muttered my mother bitterly. "They drink like pigs, they have no money for decent food. Their houses are filthy — look at her, her nose is full of rubbish. *Feh!* But to put the hair in *shmattas* — for that they have plenty of time!"

Even at my age I knew that there was something wrong with my mother's logic, but I didn't care. Nor did I care about Phyllis' nasty *goyishe* corkscrew curls or her snot-encrusted Irish nose. Phyllis could look down the centre of flowers and see palaces and gardens, and she had taught me how to do it too. I'd wait in a corner of our garden and Phyllis would bring me a skirtful of flowers. We'd peer down their stems and tell each other what we saw. I saw lords and ladies and velvet gowns and glittering jewels and lawns and mansions. Sometimes I caught sight of endlessly turning corridors. They looked as if they could go on forever.

The girl who sat next to me in 5A once gave me a chocolate shirt for my birthday. It was wrapped in cellophane and was the same size as a real shirt. It had frosted yellow buttons down the front, a white sugar handkerchief whose points stuck out from the breast pocket, and a natty polka-dotted bow tie. I loved my chocolate shirt with a passion, but after a few days my delight turned to resentment. The shirt had thrown me into a panic. What was I to do with it? The thought of sinking my teeth into the velvety chocolate filled me with a mixture of longing and dread. How could I spoil it with my greed? Each day I'd hurry home from school and stare at the shirt, my mouth drooling. Once, I even ripped a corner of the cellophane and licked one of the buttons. It smudged. Then I stuffed it into the back of a drawer and tried to forget it. Weeks later, I woke up in the middle of the night, grabbed the shirt and tore the cellophane right off. It had gone all white and mouldy. I gobbled it up in one go. Dead chocolate.

My father was a gifted cougher. He earned this accolade by smoking about seventy-five cigarettes a day. Watching him cough was a terrifying experience. The cough would start off mildly enough but just as you thought it was about to fizzle out, it would escalate into a full-scale choking fit. Feivel's face would mottle, his eyes pop out on stalks, his veins knot into purple ropes. It was obvious to anyone watching him that he was about to die. We would all stare in horrified fascination, helpless to do anything. And then, just when we had given up all hope, the coughing would stop, my father's face would gradually return to its normal mild expression and he would fish out another cigarette and light up.

Besides Yom Kippur, Passover was the one ceremony we all observed in our family. Aunty Milly laid the table with care and reverence — the bitter herbs, the burnt egg, the honey and apple. The richly embroidered three-layered matzoh cover was brought out from its year-old hibernation. A gleaming bowl with a fresh white monogrammed towel was laid to one side of my grandfather's throne-chair. Apart from the regular family settings, two extra places were laid. One was for Elijah the Prophet, the Honoured Guest, at whose place stood an elaborately chased silver goblet, the best the family had. The other place was for Bubba who, like the matzoh cover, also emerged from her year-long hibernation for this one event.

We sat around the festive Pesach table, my whole family and my great-grandmother who on this most different of all nights was safely and discreetly trussed up like an old chook, the pus wiped away from the eye socket, the yellowed hair scraped back into a knotty little bun. It occurred to me that since it was not a Friday, my aunt must have paid Bubba a discreet Passover visit. I wasn't too sure of the significance of Passover, but Bubba's presence at the table guaranteed that it was a function apart from all other functions, one to be regarded with awe and reverence.

I covered myself in glory as usual by my flawless recital of the Four Kashas. My grandfather struck dread into my heart by his darkly dramatic chanting of the Ten Plagues. For each one the red wine was spilt, splotching, as if with blood gouts, the whiteness of the plate — *Dam. . .Svardeyah . . .Kinim. . .Arov. . .* , the last and worst of all — *Makat b'choyroth* — rolling off his patriarchal tongue like a stone.

Then arrived the moment I had been dreading — inviting Elijah to partake of our feast. To the adults it may have been a symbolic act; to me it was only too real. Somewhere out in that murky corridor which led into my Aunty Milly's flat lurked some bearded hook-nosed old Hebrew. He was probably hungry and vengeful, and furious at being kept waiting. Under his striped desert robes was hidden a long-bladed scimitar which I knew he would use on me, the nearest and most helpless prey.

In fear and trembling, I opened the door and called into the corridor the words my grandfather had taught me: "Eliahu Hanavi. Eliahu Hanavi. . . . " No one answered, but I felt a hostile and alien presence in the shadows. My family, a few yards behind me, sitting around the cozy table in a warm web of domesticity, seemed millions of miles away. "Eliahu Hanavi," I whispered again, hoping that he wouldn't hear me and, if he did, wouldn't accept the invitation. Nobody answered. I quickly slammed the door and scuttled back inside.

Now the service is over, the food eaten, and we're coming to the part we enjoy most of all — the singing of the special Passover songs. We're all relaxed. Smiling. All, that is, except my mother. She sits unyielding, her mouth pursed into a tight knot, an ugly ridge of discontent between her eyes. More than anything else I want her to be happy. She refuses to please me; she refuses to please herself. When the whole table sings and my hostile divided family seems for one brief moment to have attained a picture-book serenity, won't my mother surrender her misery, if only for this night? On this festival of Passover, when the Angel of Death at God's behest passed over his unique angelic function, cannot Fanya pass over her unique human function, her special gift for misery? Must she get up from the table so abruptly and disappear into the back bedroom?

"Mummy," I plead through the shut door. "Come back to the table. Let's sing. Let's have a good time."

"Leave me alone," she replies through tight lips. "I have a headache, that's all."

"But come back and sing." I can hear the whine in my voice. "Everybody's singing. Why aren't you? Your headache will go away, I promise."

"Get away and leave me by myself. If I wanted to be with everybody, I would be. I want to be here. Go away! I'm all right! I'm all right. . . . "

The strain in these words is obvious. But I don't have the authority, the confidence, to say, No, mother, you're lying. You're not all right. You're all wrong. You're all mixed up, and you're mixing me up too!

I return to the table. My aunts and uncles are singing at the top of their voices, their eyes sparkling with warmth and affection. My father sits wrapped in his own private thoughts, a secret smile on his face. The smile is not for me. God, I think, why does *he* have to be my father? Why does *she* have to be my mother? It's not fair! I'd rather have even

Aunty Milly. At least from her I get rags. . . .

Scene: I'm in the backyard with snot-nosed Phyllis, looking down the throats of flowers. Suddenly a blood-curdling scream from the kitchen. I freeze to the spot. Thelma, my nanny, appears at the back door, her hands clasped in front of her. She holds up her right hand as if to wave at me. Her middle finger is hanging from a thin thread of gristle. Blood spurts from it in huge clotting blobs. "Look, pet," she says, and there's almost a playful tone to her voice. "Look what I've done to my finger."

I faint. When I come to, Nanny has gone. My mother has already advertised for "another girl." I don't want another girl, I want Nanny. She had been chopping herring by the window and a bird had swooped by and distracted her. I try to understand how one small bird who happened to be flying by could cause such changes in my life; how one swoop of a chopper could cut off from me forever somebody I depend on, somebody I need. But Nanny's finger is gone. Nanny is gone. Something has come to an end in my small desperate life.

Our parents put Carlton and me together in their double bed when they went to parties, because they thought it was cute, just like our joint birthday parties. I didn't mind being put to bed with Carlton. True, he was fat and milky-white, but he was almost as clever as I was and knew many more stories. We used to talk in bed for hours, and giggle until one of us — usually fat Carlton — peed the bed.

One night we stopped talking. Carlton jumped out of bed — we were in his house — and took out some twigs and sticks and pebbles from his pants pocket. He laid them down carefully on the sheet and stared at me. Somehow I knew what he expected me to do. I pulled up my flannel nightie and parted my legs. Solemnly, carefully, Carlton shoved every pebble and twig into my hole. The sticks wouldn't fit. They hurt too much, although he kept trying to push them in anyhow. For some reason I didn't get angry about the pain he was causing me — I just brushed his hand aside gently whenever he got too rough. His forehead was wet with perspiration. . . .

Once Carlton discovered the fascinating hole between my legs there was no stopping us. Our parents were beside themselves. We were no longer cute. They'd surprise us behind doors, on the sofa, behind the bushes. One day they caught us under the table when they were playing cards with two other couples. I don't know why we chose that spot. Maybe the danger of being discovered excited me more than Carlton's flabby little dick. After he'd unfastened all the tricky buttons, it would fall out of his fly like a piece of left-over pie dough. Is that what our parents were carrying on about? That little wad of putty that he pressed tremblingly up against the tight space between my legs, his eyes screwed up in effort, his hair stuck to his perspiring forehead in deep and furious concentration.

Not that I got any pleasure out of all this, and neither, I'm sure, did Carlton. We must have been driven into it by some instinctive urgency to press flesh against flesh. Our parents were equally drawn and driven to frustrate our urgency, but they couldn't keep us away from each other. Finally — whether on account of this or not, I never did find out — Carlton and his parents moved away to another part of town.

Going to bed each night was torture. Terrible self-inflicted torture. First I said my prayers, which even then I recognized as being soppy:

> In my little bed I lie
> Heavenly Father hear my cry
> Lord protect me through the night
> Keep me safe till morning light. . . Amen.

After that came the torture. I had to name *everybody* — including animals — whom I had encountered throughout my entire life. Those I failed to name were doomed not to survive the night. Sometimes it took me hours to go through the list properly. If I left out a name, I'd have to start all over again from the beginning. . . .

———◆———

Monny lived in Callan Park. In my family, Callan Park were words that you did not say clearly. If you had to say them, you mumbled apologetically, as if the sound could conjure up the dread reality. Callan Park was the loony bin, the insane asylum. Jews didn't go there because they never went crazy or had nervous breakdowns. Not in Australia.

Callan Park was for the *goyim* except that Monny wasn't a *goy*. He was a Jew, a friend of my father's. When he was allowed out on weekend passes he'd always make for our house because he had no family of his own and he loved my father whose habit of silence carried a promise of acceptance.

My mother barely tolerated him. Not only was he "funny in the head" but he was repulsive. His eyes, tiny slits of sadness, sank back into his skull; his nose was huge and hooked, with nostrils which curled back to reveal acres of slimy bristles.

But it was Monny's chin which was the most gruesome. It was as long as the rest of his face — perhaps longer — and it seemed to have a life of its own. I don't think this bothered Monny. In fact, I think he considered his chin to be his best feature because he was forever stroking and caressing it.

One of the reasons my mother hated Monny's presence was that he was a holdover from my father's bachelor days. She was always hinting, in the hapless Monny's presence, that if not for the gift of marriage she had so generously bestowed on Feivel, he too would have ended up in Callan Park. But Feivel defended Monny when Fanya attacked him. "He's my friend," he repeated whenever Fanya threw a tantrum at the prospect of another visit. "And he's always welcome in my house. Always." His tone, for once, was firm, and my mother, sensing defeat, retreated. So Monny continued to visit and he and my father would go for long walks in Centennial Park, returning in the evening when Fanya begrudgingly served them dinner.

In the last few months of her pregnancy with me, my mother became obsessed with Monny's chin. She was convinced that if her glance lingered on him, the child inside her would develop a chin just like his. In fact, for a time she believed that she had an ugly viola-chinned Monny sitting, like a homunculus, inside her, and she took to her bed weeping and thrashing around and tearing at her protruding belly whenever Monny appeared. Finally he was banned from the house until her confinement was safely over, even though that meant he no longer had any place to go for weekend leave and had to spend his free time with the *meshugenas*.

After I was born, pretty as a picture and with a perfectly proportioned chin, my father once more asserted his will and Monny was gradually allowed back. I remember him dandling me on his knees. I didn't learn of my mother's obsession till much later and when I did, I began to feel guilty for causing his banishment. I would look furtively in mirrors, taking my chin in my hands, waggling it from side to side. I even started measuring it with a tape, from my lower lip to the tip. According to the tape, my chin grew a good inch every time it was measured. . . .

So a curse had been laid on me, the gifted fairy-child, after all. Despite all precautions, despite banning the wicked wizard from the enchanted castle, there was no escaping one's fate. . . .

Evidence of My Sadistic Nature

Example one: After Carlton left, Blanchie came to live next door. She was two years younger than myself, a scrawny child with mouse-brown hair and crossed eyes. I had to walk her to school every morning because she was new and timid and Jewish and our parents were friends. Her timidity and ugliness brought out a sadism in me I was only dimly aware of. Each school morning as soon as we were out of sight of our homes, I would Chinese-burn her all the way to the school grounds. When the time came for us to part for our different classes, the flesh on her arm would be patterned in scarlet welts. In between the Chinese-burn treatment, I'd sweet-talk her and promise her I'd never do it again. Even though I was ashamed and disgusted — even frightened — at what I was doing, I knew I'd do it again. Poor Blanche. She was held in a reign of terror, petrified of even greater tortures if she were to breathe a word to her parents. For how long this went on I can't remember. What I can remember is the look of helpless bird-like panic as I came to pick her up each morning, and the way she learnt to hold out her pathetic little arm as a sacrificial offering to the cruel god-like power I possessed.

Poor little Blanche. I sometimes think of her. Does she ever think of me? Does she bear the emotional scars of my inexplicable behaviour even now — or has it become a trivial non-memory, part of the inescapable unfairness of being a child at the mercy of a neurotic world? She's probably a well-adjusted matron, scrupulously fair and loving with her children. I'm the one who has borne the scars.

More Evidence of My Sadistic Nature

Example two: I'm in my mother's kitchen. She's at the stove making soup. She has just lifted a hunk of meat from the boiling water on the stove and placed it on the table behind her. On the table is a cabbage. Nestled in one of its leaves is a small velvety green caterpillar. With great gentleness I take the caterpillar and place it on top of the hunk of steaming meat. It twitches and coils, writhes and somersaults, does a mad little frenzied tango. I hate it. I love it. Tenderly I lift it off, blow air on it and put it back onto its nice cool green cabbage leaf. Then when I have gauged as closely as I can that its dim-witted caterpillar brain has forgotten its hellish experiences, I lift it off — again with the same tender concern — and flick it back onto the hunk of boiling-hot meat. Immediately it goes into its "danse macabre."

I repeat this sequence seven or eight times, each time with immense satisfaction, until, finally, when I put it back on the meat, it remains still and seems to drain of all its colour right in front of my eyes. "Mum, there's a dead caterpillar on the meat," I say calmly. My mother goes berserk. Her soup is ruined, she shrieks. So is her day. So is her life. The familiar escalation of my mother's hysteria makes me feel good, gives me a strange sense of satisfaction. Instead of feeling helpless as I usually do, I feel calm, in control.

The arching caterpillar, the cracked white plate with the greyish hunk of meat, the aromatic steam, my mother's shrieks, the delicate green of the innocent cabbage — I close my eyes and the scene comes back to me again. Comes back and freezes, so that I can feel again what I felt then — a mysterious sense of well-being and satisfaction at the essential rightness of that grotesque episode. And then Blanche's scrawny red-wealed arm intrudes into the picture, cuts across it — and I shiver and cry and begin to hate myself all over again.

The Eye in the Box

Scene: I'm looking down the front of my bottle-green woollen bathing suit. I'm looking to see if my nipples are still there. Someone told me that wool irritates nipples so much they drop off. I don't really believe that this is true, yet I almost expect to find them, looking like little pink and brown scalloped shells, caught up in the fold of my swimsuit.

What will my sprouting breasts look like without their nipples? Will they look like two white blind moons? Will they have raw runny holes in them? This time, when I check, everything's in place, but who knows what will happen next time? Maybe my nipples won't be caught up in the folds of my bathers — maybe they'll have dropped into the sand and disappeared among the thousands of other little scalloped shells. When the cold night comes, there they'll be, shrivelled and dried up. Lost forever.

The highest accolade in the entire universe my mother could give anyone was to say, "She's so clean I could eat off her floors." Visions of my mother on her hands and knees, mouth bared to gobble slops off the shiny hard shellacked boards. Like a dog. Like a hyena. She throws her head back from time to time and looks at me, skeins of saliva swaying from the sides of her mouth. "Do it, Annale, do it. It's good to have a floor so clean you can eat off it. It's good! Do it!" And then she's on to me. Claws fastened to the back of my neck, forcing my head down to the boards. My nose pressed against the hardness of the floor; my mouth pressed against the pale soapy slops. . . .

For my mother, pleasure was always in the past tense. "That was a delicious meal, wasn't it?" she would remark when we were dining in a restaurant, less than halfway through the main course, with the dessert still to come. Or we'd be watching a movie with the final mystery about to unravel. "Wasn't that a terrific film?" my mother would say brightly. She'd gather up gloves, bags, jackets, start rummaging around for fares in her handbag, her feet shuffling with impatience.

I'd fill up with a puzzled anger but I was never able to articulate — either to her or to myself — that the pleasure was still with me, that I was holding it in my grasp right at that moment, and that her impatience was wresting it away from me.

My mother always hid from me in crowded places, dodging into doorways, stepping behind escalators, crouching behind display cases. I knew from experience that it was only a game, that I was not really abandoned. But inevitably, after the first few minutes of looking around frantically, of trying to fight off the waves of panic, I began to sob out loudly in the anonymous crowd, "Mummy! I've lost my mummy!"

Only when my sobbing had reached a frantic crescendo did my mother appear, all smiles, to hug me and chide me for being so silly. "It was just a game, you foolish little thing," she'd say with a fond teasing tone in her voice, a tone which I detected only on those occasions. "You didn't really think I'd lose you, did you?"

I'd cling to her, frightened and confused. "Please don't play that game again, Mummy. Please don't," I'd beg. But I knew, even as I pleaded with her, that she derived far too much pleasure from the game ever to abandon it.

There were two things in my house that I was afraid of — besides my mother, that is. One was my great-grandmother's glass eye. For some obscure reason, my mother inherited it when Bubba died. Even more obscure were her reasons for keeping it. It lay in the top left-hand drawer of her dressing table, under her bras and panties, in a small black box with an elastic band around it. I found it there one day when I was rummaging among Fanya's things. I thought it might have been a specially valuable piece of jewellery set aside from the mother-of-pearl inlaid box which sat on top of her dresser. When I opened it, full of expectations, my great-grandmother's green eye stared balefully up at me from its bed of cotton wool. There were even a few little red veins, for "natural effect," I guess. I was horrified. Frozen with disgust and fear. But I was drawn to that box, and often when my mother wasn't around I opened it, my heart beating in anticipation. I stared at it and it stared back at me.

Bubba's eye.

The other thing I was afraid of was the photo of my paternal grandmother in her coffin. It was kept on the top shelf of the bedroom wardrobe. My grandmother, whom I had never known (my father's family had emigrated to Canada) lay in her coffin. Her face was bound in some sort of heavy bandage, and the rest of her was covered in what appeared to be a white silk shawl with the Star of David embroidered on it. Her face looked very stern.

Standing in a semi-circle around the top of the coffin were my father's brothers. Like my father, they were small and thick-set. They were dressed in dark three-piece suits and black homburg hats. Their size and the way they were arranged around the coffin reminded me of the dwarves around Snow White's bier. The scene filled me with horror.

Why did those five awful little brothers send such a photo to my father? And why, like Bubba's glass eye, did my mother keep it?

Scene: My father is reading the newspaper in the living room. I'm opposite, watching. I go over and flick the sheets of the paper with my thumb and middle finger. Flick them hard so that they almost jump onto my father's reading glasses. There is no reaction. I move back to my seat. I watch. Again I move across the room. Flick. Nothing. Flick. This time much harder. Nothing. FLICK! This time I practically shove my fingers through the newspaper into his eyes. Success! He lowers the pages and stares at me in mild surprise. I retreat, thoroughly satisfied.

Variations on scene: My father is sitting in his armchair, staring out of the window. He is thinking. A book lies open on his lap. I take a flying leap across the room and stomp on his slippered toes. No reaction. I retreat. Again a flying leap, a grinding stomp on his toes. There's no reaction, not even a grimace. I don't retreat this time. I stay where I am and stomp and stomp and stomp on my father's toes. I grind them into the floor with my heels. I press down with all my strength. Victory! My father, in slow motion, reaches back for a cushion and gently throws it at me. I've broken through into his fortress, his barricade of books. I'm ecstatic.

Sometimes Feivel emerged from behind his silence and told me about his past and how he had been a Bolshevik and fought in the Revolution. Once the cossacks came looking for him. They were after the piles of revolutionary pamphlets which he printed and distributed in secret. Luckily the household was alerted and my grandmother, who ran a bakery, grabbed huge fistfuls of the incriminating papers and stuffed them into the oven.

By the time the first cossack had splintered open the front door there was nothing left of the evidence but a handful of ashes. My father had already fled and was on his way out of the country to Palestine. With a similar group of ghetto exiles, he took back-breaking work, shovelling sand and clearing stones from a tract of sun-baked desert. When they had cleared the site, they were told that there was no money to pay them for their labours. They could, however, lay claim to some of the stony desert they had just finished clearing. Jeers. Laughter. Everyone walked away cursing, except for the two or three who, out of desperation, took up the offer. Since the land my father had hauled and broken stones on was to become Tel Aviv, they later became millionaires. Needless to say, my father was not one of them. Instead, he got a job as a deckhand on a boat going to Australia. He wanted to get away from the rest of the world, far away from the pogroms and ghettos and cossacks and stone breaking.

What my father found when he jumped boat in Sydney was my mother.

My Aunty Milly got cancer of the lower bowel and had to have a colostomy — that is, she had to shit through an artificially made hole in her side. Not really a hole. It was

54

more like a huge swollen purple nipple. I know because I made her show it to me. Lots of times. Another useless nipple on my poor aunty's useless body. Around her hips she wore a sort of harness which held a plastic cup in place over the unreliable hole.

All of a sudden the world became full of colostomy jokes, colostomy people.

Question: Why did the prostitute ask the doctor to give her a colostomy?

Answer: So she could make some money on the side.

Clark Gable had a colostomy. President Roosevelt. And Jan Peerce, the opera singer. So did Queen Mary — that's why she always pursed her lips so tightly; she was nervous she'd let out a huge fart in the middle of reviewing the Household Cavalry. And Raisel Chorley, wife of the Chairman of the Combined Jewish Appeal, had one. "Do you know," whispered my Aunty Sonya, "that Elizabeth Taylor has a colostomy? That's why she's always going in and out of hospitals. She's had one since she was a baby."

Elizabeth Taylor had a colostomy when she rode National Velvet to victory? But didn't the violent motion of the galloping horse jolt the plastic cup out of place? Didn't she spill shit all down the front of her impeccable English jodhpurs? I tried to persuade my Aunty Milly to imitate the galloping motion of a horse — I needed to test this notion — but something had gotten into her. The gravity of her illness had lifted her to a place beyond my bossy control. Aunty Milly was no longer my thing. She belonged to her illness. It conferred upon her an importance she'd never before had. Her family respected her colostomy more than they had ever respected her. They showered her with little luxuries — a bottle of Chanel No. 5, a French lace hankie, an alligator-skin purse.

For a while my aunt flourished. She even grew pretty. For the first time, a man — a widower in his early fifties — asked her out to dinner. Milly's very first date. Marriage of course was out of the question, murmured my aunts patronizingly, pityingly, but wasn't it nice for Milly.

And then Aunty Milly's late blooming was cut short. Her eyes receded into her head; her skin became yellow and waxy; her hair thinned. She had "secondaries" — first in her liver and then, emboldened by their success, the cells rampaged throughout her whole body. She was hospitalized. Her liver fed on her, took control of her body. Each day, each hour, while Aunty Milly grew smaller and smaller, it grew larger and larger. Just as she never existed for herself in life, so she ceased to exist for herself in death — her body served as a nourishment centre for her greedy liver.

Fanya, Queen of Pain, preempted everybody else's suffering as usual, even the victim's. Somehow she managed to turn my poor aunt's sickness into a weapon to be used against herself. She spent all her time sitting and weeping by the dying woman's bedside. At least once a week I would be dragged to the hospital to share my mother's penance. The changes were dramatic. With the sheet pulled up to her chin, Aunty Milly looked like a shrunken wax doll. Only her liver stuck up under the sheet like a huge obscene bulge, a grotesque parody of a pregnancy. She was giving birth to a giant cancer.

The gaping hole in her chest, the raised artificial anus in her side, the mound of hungry liver — she was all wrong, my Aunty Milly, her body a series of perverse convexities and concavities.

Finally she died. I remember wondering at the size of her coffin. She should have been laid like a doll in one of those toy matchboxes and buried beneath a bush in our backyard with a twig stuck on top and a little piece of paper with "Here Lies Aunty Milly" scrawled on it in childish spidery letters.

Description of Unhappy Dreams

Dream one: I see before me a huge sheet of paper. I crawl across it like a bug across an enormous screen. In my hands is a tiny stub of a pencil. I must write on the paper, scratch black marks all over its whiteness. Painfully, grotesquely, I attempt to reach the upper left-hand corner of the enormous sheet, trying to scrawl an urgent message with my microscopic stub. I am nauseous with effort, lost between a hugeness and a tininess, with me in between trying desperately to make a connection, to bring the two unconnected objects into some sort of balance.

Dream two: I find myself sitting in a shiny midget car caught in the middle of a giant black highway. Sodium lights shine garishly down on its harsh surface and I know that I must drive frantically before something horrible catches up to me.

Dream three: I'm poised over a huge bowl, huge enough to drown in. It is full of some sort of stagnant seaweedy broth. In order to go on living, I must swallow it. But I have been given — by god knows what spiteful Authority — a minute silver spoon, not large enough to hold an eye dropper full of liquid. It's even too small to hold between my clumsy fingers. I try to scoop up some liquid from the vast bowl. It is hopeless. I shall never succeed.

Dream four: My fingers have sprouted great splintered yellow-tinged nails which rip to pieces anything they touch. I have a pair of tiny, daintily ornamented scissors with which to trim them.

My night-time head is bursting with these ponderous huge-nesses, with these fly-away, doll-like tininesses. How to put the two together? How to compensate the too-muchness of one with the too-littleness of the other?. . .

When I wake up exhausted from such dreams, I have to be reassured, have to prove the world to myself. I blow my normal-sized nose into a normal-sized handkerchief; eat a normal-sized bowl of cereal with a normal-sized spoon; button and unbutton my school shirt. Button goes into hole. Button goes out of hole. In. Out. In. Out. It all works perfectly. It fits. I note with massive relief that the universe is in scale after all. And, most comforting of all, I'm in scale with it.

But each night I conspire with myself to mash my daytime certainties to a pulp. I can't take anything for granted. Every morning when I wake up, I have to re-invent the world.

My father took me to the Sydney Municipal Library. It was the first time he had taken me anywhere and I was giddy with happiness. He was letting me in on his secret world. Away from his hopeless inadequacies in the *shmatta* world, Feivel seemed strong, masterful, in control. We walked in silence through the stacks of books. "Choose a book," instructed my father, smiling at me. "Choose! They all belong to you now. Every one of them."

I reached out and plucked a book. I hardly glanced at the title. It didn't matter. What mattered was my father's attention, the calm muted sounds of pages being turned, the delicious feeling of belonging.

Holding my hand, Feivel led me to the desk. We waited until the librarian had performed her ritual — the slotting in of the cards, the soft scratching of the pen, the reassuring swoosh of the rubber stamp. When she asked for my name, my father answered for me. "Anna Cohen," he said in ringing tones. It was the first time I had heard him say it. Anna Cohen. Never had my name sounded so right.

Lokshen on the Sheet

After my father was forced by my ambitious mother to give up the barrow business, life became a series of grinding money worries. Feivel had the reverse Midas touch — everything he touched turned to dross. Thriving businesses went broke within a few months of his tender ministrations, and it didn't take too long before the word got around — keep Feivel Cohen out of it.

My mother was beside herself with worry and shame. Every day her friends were getting richer and richer; every day we were getting poorer and poorer.

"Nu, we can't all be businessmen, can we?" consoled Molly Gevurtz, who had just installed a private swimming pool in her back garden, even though neither she, her husband nor her asthmatic son ever intended to put a foot into it. "If only Feivel had stayed in the barrow game!"

If only. . . Fanya's plans had backfired with a vengeance. But Feivel was cheerfully unconcerned with making a living. To him it was an irritant, a bothersome interruption in the rhythm of his daily life.

My grandfather decided to take matters in hand and send his unsuccessful son-in-law, his discontented daughter and his disturbed granddaughter to Melbourne where he had bought "for a bargain" an almost defunct button factory. He hoped that with diligence and shrewdness — qualities which Feivel had never before exhibited in his entire life —

my father would be able to put the factory "back onto its feet."

We sold our comfortable house on Furber Road, stored the furniture, and set forth on the *Spirit of Progress* to seek fame and fortune — or at least fortune — in the Queen City of the South.

Did my grandfather think that my father, who had turned any number of living businesses into corpses in record time, could by a process of magical reversal turn a moribund business into a thriving one? Who knows? It was a desperation move and one that was bound to fail. It did. We went broke again, this time taking my hapless grandfather into financial perdition with us.

But before we returned home in disgrace to Sydney, we had to finish out our miserable year in Melbourne. No longer could we afford the pleasant flat we had been renting. My parents were forced to move to a boarding house which didn't take children, and I was farmed out to a local Jewish immigrant family who needed the money. They certainly didn't need me.

My parents should have investigated with just a little more care where it was that they were sending their daughter to live. Or maybe they wanted to give me a course in Yiddish since not one word of English was spoken in that household. *"Ich hob dir feynt,"* spat out Yudel, the five-year-old boy, the minute he laid eyes on me. He accompanied this greeting with a huge gob of spit which landed in my eye. I should have known by this that the sentiments he expressed were neither loving nor gentle, but my need for approval was so great that I translated the words into what I hoped were their closest English equivalent — "I hope you're fine." When I found out what he really meant — "I hate you" — I quickly learnt Yiddish, a language which seemed filled with curses and mocking diminutives.

I had to learn fast to defend myself in that family. The mother and father were hysterical, harassed, ignorant; the fierce-looking Zayde, tyrannical, narrow-minded and sadistic.

60

He fed Yudel and me our meals, since the parents worked in a sweat shop from early morning till late at night.

I, who had been taught that to start the day without a glass of freshly squeezed orange juice was courting certain death, was now fed strong black tea with salt herring for breakfast and dinner. Even though I was terrified of Zayde, he at least kept to his own world — I came and went on the periphery of his life like some scrawny little alley cat. It was Yudel who made hell out of my days, Yudel who would not leave me alone but vented all his five-year-old neurotic spleen on me, the lowest of the pecking order in the household. His favourite activity was to run after me in the street on my way to school, pull down his pants and piss on my shoes. Often he would pursue me as far as the school yard and piss on me again. His bladder, it seemed, was inexhaustible and able to produce massive amounts of urine at will.

Having humiliated me, he would then scuttle off home and proceed to tear up every book I possessed, or else smash in the face of whatever doll I was currently lavishing my poor starved affection on. Zayde didn't stop him. He was too busy sipping his scalding-hot tea in the poky back room and brooding bitterly on his former life.

Once for a birthday present, Aunty Bashka sent me a doll which came with a cradle and a complete set of pretty clothes. When I hurried home from school to play with my newly acquired treasure, I found the doll's face smashed into pieces, the cradle splintered, the clothes soaked in piss. I threw myself down on the floor and howled so hard I passed out from lack of oxygen. After that, my parents must have realized that I was in a state of desperate unhappiness. They collected me from that savage family and we all travelled back — our Melbourne experience a disaster — to the known and therefore secure miseries of Sydney.

After the button-factory fiasco, we returned in disgrace to a flat which was much too small to accommodate the grandly scaled furniture from our previous house. Although it was located in the well-to-do suburb of Bellevue Hill, it was cramped and jerry-built.

Without any words being spoken — at least, none that I was aware of — my father took up occupancy of the second bedroom, the one with my Three Pigs fitted coverlet, while I took his place in the mahogany double bed.

My mother tried yet again to settle my father "in business." This time it was a pleating factory — Neet-Pleet. Pleats, it seemed, were in style. No woman would be seen dead in a straight skirt. Sun-Ray, Gor-Ray. With pleats, no one could miss. No one, that is, except my father.

The "factory" consisted of a shabby sweltering room on the third floor of a rickety building in Taylor's Square. Stacks of cardboard patterns were crammed into shelves. Against a wall stood a huge rotting rusting steamer, hissing and spitting vindictively. The pleaters were my mother, my father and a fat giggly girl called Marcia who smoked incessantly. The manufacturers would send in bolts of cut cloth with pleating instructions — ten dozen Box Pleats; fifteen dozen Sun-Rays. My father would select the appropriate pattern and lay the material between the two cardboard sheets. Then he and my mother would each grab hold of an end and clump the material up in the folds. Grryk. Grryk. They'd hang on to it while Marcia tied the bundle up with greasy old rags and threw it into the steamer. When it was full, she'd bolt the door. After a time the steamer would emit a hideous shriek and Marcia would fling the door open, letting into the already sweltering room clouds of choking chemical stink. Grabbing hold of the burning-hot cardboard bundles, she'd toss them onto the table and my parents would unfold them and stack the still-hot pleated material into the manufacturers' boxes.

Most days after school I'd deliver the boxes to the skirt

factories which were within walking distance. I'd walk along
the streets with a set face, hoping I wouldn't run into any of
my friends. I hated Neet-Pleet with a passion — the chemical
fumes that stung the back of my throat and made my eyes
water; the sight of my parents, their faces green with
exhaustion, fluorescent with sweat; fat slug-girl Marcia with
her nicotined stubby hands; my mother's suppressed hysteria
which hung in the air, palpable and stinging as the chemical
fumes, and which erupted with a predictable and murderous
fury. I imagined hell to look and smell like that.

Sometimes, for some unavoidable reason, my father would
be left alone in the factory for an hour or so. Invariably
disaster would strike. My mother would return to find him
reading *Jew Süss*, oblivious of the banshee wails of the
malevolent steamer which was threatening to erupt and blast
the whole of Taylor's Square heavenwards. With a scream,
she would fling herself into the fumes of the steamer,
trying to rescue what she could. To no avail. The material
was ruined, stained through and through with chemicals. Or
she would discover that my father had chosen the wrong
pattern and what should have been ten dozen Gor-Ray came
out as ten dozen Box Pleats.

Always tragedies. I would return from my delivering
excursions, holding in my hand the dread parcel — a "return."
The material had been laid in its pattern carelessly and there
was a jagged crease, like an ugly wound, running across the
knife-like pleats.

Always my father's fault. His myopic blue eyes were
somewhere else — printing revolutionary pamphlets in Bialy-
stock, breaking stones in the Palestinian desert — anywhere
but clumping lumps of smelly cardboard together, he on one
end, Fanya on the other.

But he didn't have long to suffer. Skirt manufacturers
soon caught on that Neet-Pleet was a place to be avoided
at all costs. Business slowed down to a trickle. Marcia
was dismissed. My mother grew more and more worried.

My father grew more and more contented. Now he could sit down at the long wooden table and suck tea through sugar cubes and read and dream his way through the hot still day without any bothersome interruptions.

Scene: My grandfather has lung cancer and has been sent home from hospital to die. "Eat up your nice chicken soup, Dad," cajoles my mother. "Come on, Dad, eat it up. It's good for you. It'll make you feel better."

My grandfather clamps his mouth shut, shakes his head weakly from side to side. Is he aware that his death is only minutes away and that, in his last moments on earth, he is part of a bad Jewish joke?

"Come on, Dad. A sip, just a sip of broth."

My grandfather continues his obstinate head shaking.

I sit in a corner of the room reading *Ginger Meggs*. I look up from the comics, glad that my grandfather refuses to give in to his daughter's bullying.

Suddenly he pushes her out of the way and sits bolt upright. He opens his mouth and spews out a spongy mass of raspberry-pink tissue. It falls right into the plate of freshly made chicken soup. Plop!

My grandfather's eyes widen in surprise. The last thing he sees before he dies are the broken pieces of *lokshen* splattered over the white sheet.

I hated sleeping with my mother. I hated it. Hated her body warmth, the odour from her hair, her armpits, her crotch. I tried to cling to the edge of the bed to stop myself being engulfed, but it was impossible. The odours and warmth came washing over me like a soupy tidal wave. If I accidentally touched her skin during sleep, I'd jerk away, sickened.

When we had guests I insisted on sleeping in my own bed, feeling a vague but persistent shame that my parents didn't sleep together. After the guests had gone, my father carried me back to my mother's double bed. He wouldn't be caught spending even one night with her. Would he too have jerked away in revulsion if, during the night, his skin accidentally touched hers? The thought saddened and depressed me.

I *wanted* to see my father on top of my mother. I *wanted* to see them hugging and kissing and bouncing around in bed together. My disappointment was that I never did.

Scene: It's bed time. I'm lying in the double bed. For once it's peaceful in my home. I can hear my parents in the kitchen, talking quietly. The sun is sinking but there's a great golden shaft of it still touching the windowsill. I stare out at the sky, waiting for it to be dark. Suddenly, flashing through the air comes a banana skin. Time stops. The frame freezes. The banana skin is suspended in mid-flight. It is a golden pulsating parachute; it is a ballerina in a tulip tutu. I stare at it, transfixed. And suddenly I am flushed, flooded with an indescribable rush of ecstasy. I am so filled up with it I can hardly breathe. The magic banana skin hangs and shimmers in the air. I love the world. I love life. I love my parents. I love myself. I'm so stuffed with feeling, I can hardly contain myself. I start laughing with an incredible joy. "Anna," yells my mother from the kitchen, "how come you're still awake? Go to sleep and keep quiet. I don't want to hear a single sound from you."

The frame unfreezes. Plop goes the banana skin on the ground below.

The next morning before I go to school, I race around the back of the flats to see what I can find. Lying on the concrete is a limp, shiny old brown skin.

Scene: My mother is teetering on the ledge of the bedroom window. Three floors below is a steep drop into a sort of gully. She is swaying dangerously back and forth on the sill, holding onto the ledge of the half-opened window.

There is white matter at the corners of her mouth. "You're trying to kill me, aren't you?" she mutters behind clenched teeth. "My lovely daughter is trying to kill me. Well, I'll be a good mother — I'll help her. I'll do it myself. Quickly. You don't have to try so hard. I'll do it for you. . . "

What have I done? God in Heaven, what have I done? What has brought this frightening scene into being? *Who* has brought this frightening scene into being? The only possible answer is that I have. The caring daughter. The daughter who has driven her mother to kill herself. And what is it I have done? Refused to change my dirty pedal pushers for a clean skirt. It's true my mother asked me at least half a dozen times; it's true I refused. At first I was only half serious, but as she grew hysterical I became more determined not to change.

Now it has come to this — my mother is going to die a ghastly death because I won't change my clothes. Let her die! I will not back down.

Fanya emits a frightening gurgle and dangles one foot into the abyss. "Mummy, Mummy," I shriek. "I'll do it. I'll change. Right now. I'll change all my clothes. I'll change *me*. Only pull your foot back. I'll be a good girl from now on. Please, Mummy, just don't jump!"

A couple of years later I took my first look at that window. I don't know why I didn't think of doing it before. Copying Fanya, I climbed onto the ledge. It was wide and strong. The window frame I hung onto provided a secure hold. Just below the outside of the sill I noticed a brick projection upon which I could rest my dangling foot with no danger of falling.

I jumped down softly and left the room.

In my home, nothing was simple, nothing casual. Every act was fraught with sinister import.

I broke a saucer. It was High Tragedy. The End of the World. "Better you should have broken your right arm," cursed my mother. Or I made arrangements to meet my friends at Bondi Beach on Sunday. "Not until you've done the borders," hissed Fanya.

Those borders. They were my life's burden. Wall-to-wall was what our rich friends had. What *we* had were rugs which left at least two feet of bare floorboard all around. These boards, made of cheap plywood, were the bane of my mother's existence. In an attempt to disguise them as parquet she had them stained walnut; and every Sunday morning it was my duty to take a pail of warm soapy water and wash them free of dust.

Straddling those borders were massive lowboys and hautboys and brocaded settees — furniture from our earlier days which now looked ridiculous in the cheap little plastered box of an apartment. But the borders had to be done, those exposed pieces of board upon which it seemed my mother displaced all her obsessions. No matter what happened, Sunday mornings were devoted to The Cleaning — no Catholic could have been more rigid in his observance of Mass. There no deferring of time, no promises of a "tomorrow" or a "later" or, God forbid, a "let's leave it till next week." Picnics, outings, weekend excursions — all were subservient to the borders.

I anticipated those Sundays with dread. First, I would make sure that I woke up earlier than on regular mornings so that, while Fanya slept, I could steal a couple of hours from her and imagine that the day was actually mine. I'd sneak down the stairs to where the bright promise of the Sunday paper lay, the comic supplement hidden within its folds like a pearl in an oyster. Comics tucked under my arm, I'd grab an apple and crawl back into bed, careful as a thief not to make the slightest sound. Never did I relinquish the hope that if I was extra quiet, my mother would sleep on through the morning. I was convinced that if that miracle ever happened, then Fanya might realize that life — hers or mine — did not depend on the clinical cleanliness of our living quarters.

Nine o'clock would go by. Nine-thirty. My hopes would rise. I'd even venture a second apple, a reckless rustle of the comics. Then the name "Anna!" would split the air; and the day, which had started off like a shining crystal goblet, would shatter into a thousand sharp splinters.

When, after two or three hours, I'd finally finish my task, my mother would come after me for an inspection. Invariably she would find a ball of dust, a particle of ash, a twist of cotton. And then I'd be done for. Cursing and screaming, Fanya would roll on the floor. I'd stare at her, my heart hammering, the pulse in my forehead thrumming.

And that would be the end of it — my golden Sunday. The whole day lay ahead of me in ruins. An overlooked fluffball was sufficient evidence of my desire to ruin my mother, to give her cancer, to kill her. Deep down in my gut I sensed that she was right.

The Cheese Stands Alone

Scene: I'm standing in line in the school yard. It is an achingly beautiful spring day. The whistle has been blown for us to fall into line and when we "settle down and stop fidgeting" and "button up our mouths" then the next whistle will blow and we'll march indoors. All of a sudden I'm outside myself. I'm standing at a distance of at least six feet looking at myself and I'm very very happy with what I see. I'm wearing a freshly laundered blue dirndl, the sort which buttons all the way down, with an elasticized waist and puffed sleeves. It has scenes from Snow White printed on it. It's crisp and pretty and fresh, just like the spring day. Just like me. And I have a satiny pink ribbon around my blonde hair. It is tied with a soft floppy bow on the top of my head. I'm such a pretty little girl with my long blonde shiny hair and my china-blue eyes and my smooth brown skin and my strong chubby legs. It makes me feel good to look at myself. . . .

But just as suddenly I'm back inside my body. Really inside. I'm underneath my pretty cotton dirndl, underneath my soft brown skin. I'm right in the middle of my intestines. Dark. Purple-red. Wet. Shiny. Glistening. Undulating. Pulsing. Sucking. I try to get out. Waves of nausea engulf me.

When I come to, I'm lying on a couch in the nurse's office. She tells me that I fainted. "It must have been the sun," she says in her matter-of-fact way, and lays a cool efficient finger on my racing pulse.

Scene: We're all standing in the playground under the shade of a jacaranda tree. It's "outdoors-activity time" and Miss Herlihy has arranged us all in a circle to play "The Farmer in the Dell." Dickie Cassidy is chosen to be the farmer. He takes Jennifer Leckey to be his wife. Jennifer takes Lurline Snell. Lurline takes Pam, Pam takes Barry. I'm sweating with tension because I know what's going to happen. The game continues. The dog takes a cat, the cat takes a rat. The rat is Neil Waters. He skips around the circle slowly. He's pretending to think about who the cheese is going to be, but I know he's already decided. He stops in front of me.

> The cheese stands alone,
> The cheese stands alone,
> Hi ho the derry-o,
> The cheese stands alone.

Everyone in the circle is pointing at me. They're clapping and stamping their feet. I don't want to be the cheese. I don't want to stand alone. It's not fair. Scalding tears prick my eyes and my chest begins to heave. I look over at Miss Herlihy. She's looking back at me. Smiling. There's a spiteful gleam in her beady little eyes.

Remembrance Day. Another *goyishe* ritual. Another solemn occasion whose significance escaped me entirely. Remembrance Day was the worst ordeal of all, the day when everybody had to shut up for two minutes and think of the sacrifices made by "our boys." I didn't know who "our boys" were, let alone the sacrifices they were supposed to have made. I thought they must be vaguely related to Jesus because I was always being told at school that he also made a sacrifice on my behalf, the significance of which also escaped me. The solemn drone of "God of Our Fathers" filled me with a bleak foreboding.

Still stands Thine ancient sacrifice
    An humble and a contrite heart
Lord God of Hosts be with us yet
    Lest we forget, lest we forget.

What was "an humble and a contrite heart"? An "ancient sacrifice"? I was convinced, as usual, that everybody in the world knew, except me. I flashed on to an image in my history book of an Aztec priest on top of a pyramid holding up a dripping heart to the sun god, although how that related to the dreary dirge I was mouthing, I couldn't quite work out. One thing I did know for sure, though — the Lord God of Hosts had nothing, absolutely nothing, to do with me. Nor did I wish him to. I fervently desired to keep as much distance as possible between that "awful hand" and myself. My overriding concern on Remembrance Day was to remember not to draw attention to myself, not to bring down upon my defenceless head the wrath of principals, peers and that terrible, avenging God.

But the songs weren't the hardest part. It was the silence that killed me. I always started off all right, except that never once did I think of "our boys." Instead, I wondered what sort of a mood my mother would be in when I got home; I plotted how to get out of gym; I agonized over whether I'd lost my front door key yet again.

All this took about half a minute and then I was left with a yawning chasm of one and a half minutes. Unfortunately, I knew only too well from former unhappy experiences how I was going to fill them — I was going to laugh. It would start off as a tiny trembly bubble until finally it would burst into a huge resounding yawp.

I looked around me surreptitiously. Everybody else's eyes were properly downcast, their faces obedient masks of sadness and sobriety. There was no doubt that they were thinking the right thoughts. The only infidel in the entire assembly was me. The Jewess. The barbarian. I began to shake. My eyes filled with tears of hysteria. My doom was sealed. Again I'd be sent to the principal. Again I'd be accused of heartlessness, of insensitivity, of callousness. But I was helpless to avert my certain fate. I opened my mouth and a shriek of uncontrollable laughter escaped. Miss Herlihy — the dreaded Miss Herlihy — glared and beckoned. . . .

Scene: Monday morning. Assembly time. I always feel horrible in assembly. It heightens my already sharp sense of isolation. It's not quite as bad as Remembrance Day but it comes around much more often. First we all come trooping into the assembly hall — sweaty little Australian school children — to the cool and measured strains of "In an English Country Garden." *La-la-dee da-da, la-dee-da-dee-dum — in an English country ga-ar-den.* . . .

What on earth an English country garden actually looks like, nobody knows. One thing we *do* know, though — it can have nothing at all in common with the heat-shimmering asphalt in the playground, where a few rhododendron bushes wilt in one corner, a dusty laburnum bush languishes in the other, and a Moreton Bay fig drops its sticky fruits onto the prickly yellow grass.

Nor do we care. We're much more concerned about trying to catch a glimpse of the iridescent rainbows which circle the armpits of Mrs. Stove's blue serge dress. They flash out at us whenever she raises her arms from the piano to pound out another chord.

When we are all in place we have a flag ceremony, with the smug prissy prefects (oh, how I wish that I were one!) holding up the Southern Cross — "I love my God; I honour my King; I salute (and here a solemn pause for grubby hands to be held to sweaty foreheads) my flag."

I know it's all a bunch of hogwash but since everyone looks so serious and absorbed, I don't say a word. My thoughts, though, are busy. How can they love a god who is idiot enough to have for a son such a watery-eyed, pearly-toothed, golden-curled simpering ninny dressed in a nightie! Such a goy! "My King" is another goy — one who stutters to boot. A weak wishy-washy *gornisht* with a wife whose tits hang down to the ground and two muddy-faced little goody-goodies for daughters.

I nurse a strong and unshakeable conviction that the entire Royal Family suffers from chronic constipation, and when I think of the King at all — which is seldom — I picture him sitting on a solid-gold toilet, his face under his bejewelled crown white and strained from the effort of producing one mean hard little turd. . . .

Scene: It's assembly time again. We're standing in obedient rows. Mrs. Stove is pounding out the chorus of "All Things Bright and Beautiful."

> All things bright and beautiful
> > All creatures great and small
> All things wise and wonderful
> > The Lord God made them all.

I'm mad about that song. It makes *me* feel bright and beautiful, although, as usual, the inclusion of the Lord God spoils things.

The sun is splashing into the assembly room. It falls across my white elasticized socks and my new shiny red patent-leather shoes, making them wink. A stab of pure joy shoots through me. Somebody — it doesn't matter who — is in his heaven, and all's right with the world.

Suddenly with no warning, the girl behind, Deirdre her name is, leans against me and, with a groan, throws up all over my shiny new shoes. Yellow, orange and dark-brown vomit. Lumpy. Hot. Smelly.

Each little flower that opens
Each little bird that sings
He made their glowing colours
He made their tiny wings.

Did He also make Deirdre's vomit? I ask myself as the nauseating steamy stench rises to meet my nostrils.

Scene: I've gotten an early mark. I'm the best reader, so to reward me the teacher sends me out of the only class I really enjoy, with a ten-minute "early mark." I'm exiled, marooned in an empty playground. I wander around aimlessly. Next door to the playground is a church with a graveyard. People are gathered around an empty hole. I sneak through the wooden slats of the fence and hang around the fringe of the group. The coffin is standing by the grave, waiting to be lowered. All of a sudden I remember something that somebody once told me — "Dead bodies stink." An almost palpable stink seems to emanate from underneath the closed lid of the coffin. At first it's faint, a mere shadow of a smell, an elusive whiff as of some metallic substance. Then it becomes stronger and sharper until I feel I'm going to faint. A dense heavy clotted odour, a sharp stink of decaying animal, of corrupting flesh. Sickened, I dive back into the playground. The others are just beginning to flood out for lunch. "Lucky thing," they say, their voices glutinous with envy. "Jeez, you're a lucky thing. Early mark an' all. . . . "

"Please, Miss, may I go across the yard?" This was what we all had to say if we wanted to use the toilet. This phrase and no other contained the magic formula. No matter that "Miss" was actually a "Mrs.," that the toilets were not across the yard (they were, in fact, just down the hall). It was what you had to say if you wanted to pee outside the permitted time.

"Why didn't you make your visit at play time?" asked the teacher, thin-lipped with disapproval. Did she really mean me to answer? Was there an answer? I jiggled from foot to foot unable to produce a reason why my bladder was not obedient to the rhythm of the school bells.

"If I let you go, then everyone will want to go, won't they?" continued the teacher. Against this irrefutable piece of logical madness I again remained silent. I had images in my head, though, of hordes of maddened school girls stampeding through the halls until they reached the haven of the toilets, where, finally letting go, they pissed gallons of golden pee which engulfed the whole school in an enormous tidal wave.

I was a member of the Thousand Voice Choir. One thousand Sydney girls from schools all over the city. We practised separately for six months and then came together for a final rehearsal before our performance at the Town Hall.

One thousand dewy little vaginas, some of us bleeding,

some of us not. All of us dressed in white. We sang like angels. We looked like angels. All, that is, except me. I didn't have a white dress. Although it was partly white, it had a jaunty red-and-white striped top. Nine hundred and ninety-nine snowy white virgins and one spoiled scarlet woman.

I had begged my mother to get me a pure white dress. "*Feh*," she spat. "A special dress that you'll never wear again? And for what, may I ask? To learn the violin from your own Uncle Misha — that wasn't good enough. Oh no! But to sing some *chazerai* about that anti-Semite who hangs like an idiot from the cross — *that's* good enough!"

That *chazerai*, Fanya, was Handel's Hallelujah chorus, and when I sang it I felt as if my head was lifting right off my shoulders. I felt as if my heart was going to burst out of my chest, as if my voice was going to sprout wings and swoop right out of my mouth like a white falcon. That's what that *chazerai* meant to me, Fanya. But of course I didn't say that. What I did tell her, to soften her objections, was that besides the song about Jesus we were also going to sing "Drip drip drop little April showers" and a special song by a home-grown composer:

The bush was drear a week ago
    Olive green and brown and grey
But now the spring has come this way
    With blo-o-o-ossom for the wa-aa-tle!

That only made it worse. Now the insults of the *goyishe* songs were compounded by the Australian *goyishe* songs. I could see that it was hopeless. I would not get my white dress.

When the night arrived we assembled backstage half an hour before the performance. Everybody — *everybody* — was dressed in white — pristine white. I wore a cardigan slung casually around my shoulders. Even though it was nearly 100 degrees, I made an elaborate pretence of shivering.

Mrs. Stove spotted me immediately. "Take that cardigan off this instant, Anna!"

I stood revealed, a barber pole in a white field, a vulgar red poppy in a circle of graceful lilies.

"I'll deal with you later," she snapped as she plucked me out, noxious weed that I was. I was barred from going on stage. From the desolation of the wings, I heard a great wave of applause. Muffled coughs. A discreet rustle of programs. The downward swoop of the baton.

The Thousand Voice Choir — now a misnomer because of me — opened its collective mouth. "Hallelujah! Hallelujah! Halley-loo-ya. . . . " I stood to the side. Devastated. Silent. Shut out.

Scene: A knock at the front door. When I open it I see a careworn woman with dullish red hair standing there. We look at each other in silence and then she opens her arms to me, this strange woman.

"Nanny!" I throw myself at her, sobbing and laughing and yelling. Fanya comes to the door and invites her in for a cup of tea.

Nanny is married now and has a daughter of her own. She is named after me, Annabelle. "Isn't that a pretty name?" murmurs my mother in condescending tones.

After a few minutes of forced conversation, we are all embarrassed. There is nothing more to say. I notice that Thelma really does have an atrocious Australian accent and that her dentures are even more poorly made than I had remembered. We say good-bye to each other stiffly. When she extends her right hand to me, I see an ugly discoloured stump where the middle finger should have been.

Enter Miss Frilly Pants

Scene: My mother kneels before me, twiddling ineptly, trying to slot the gauze end of the napkin through the little metal teeth of the sanitary belt. As usual when my mother comes close to me I can feel the nervous vibrations pulsing from her like tickings from a time bomb. She looks, Fanya, like an acolyte engaged in some supplicating rite to an all-powerful goddess — me. The Goddess of the Eternal Flux. Hardly anything is coming out, though. No rich-red rivers of blood, only some smudgy brown stains. It looks as if someone's shoved a Cadbury's chocolate bar up my hole and it's slowly melting into my panties, into the unfamiliar wad of cotton wool and gauze which is packed tight between my thighs. It even smells a little like chocolate — a warm, gooey, sickly, sweetish odour.

I touch the brown stains and then tentatively put my finger to my mouth and lick it — it tastes a little like chocolate too. Even the squeamishness which I'm beginning to feel in my abdomen has a sweetish cast to it.

I ask my mother for the precise time, the precise date. I'm convinced that every month for the rest of my life I shall commence bleeding at exactly the same moment. "This date will rule my life," I say to Fanya, who is still on her knees fiddling with the belt. She thinks I have said "This date will *ruin* my life." "No, no — don't ever think that.

You're a little woman now. Your life is ahead of you. It's a good thing. You should be proud of it."

About menstruation, my mother is an understanding, wise and patient liberal. But she just doesn't understand how I feel. I feel pleased — pleased and powerful and vulnerable all at the same time. I'm now in possession of a whole new power play. All I have to say to Fanya from now on is — "I've got my period." It's an intimacy I can rely on to draw instant sympathy from her. "I've got my period. . . . " The magic words will even get me off doing the dread borders.

"Anna is having trouble with her period," writes Fanya in a note to school. I'm excused from gym, no questions asked. I'm allowed to leave the classroom at any time and lie on the bamboo chaise longue outside the nurse's office, looking mysterious and pathetic.

But being pleased wears off. The excitement of confiding in friends wanes. What remains is a chafing smelly lump of cotton wool between the legs. What remains is the agony of pulling sticky blood-matted pubic hairs away from the caked pad. What remains is the rancid sweet stench. Horrible! Yech!

I've been warned by my mother and aunts about what happens if I take a bath "at that time of the month" — the blood will go to my head. I'm so devastated by this piece of information that I'm even scared to wash my hands and face in case a drop of water splashes onto my body.

When I go out for a walk, will everyone smell me? Will everyone see the bulky outline of the pad through my pedal pushers? When I get up from a sitting position, will I have soaked through onto the upholstered chair? Will a large crimson stain appear on the back of my white shorts? A new anxiety to add to the dream of walking naked down a crowded street. Will people snicker behind my back when I say I can't go swimming?

I catch myself looking out for other women. Who, in the bus, is menstruating? Right now. Right this instant. Sitting there looking demure and respectable and self-contained but actually bleeding like a stuck pig.

And the big question — do men menstruate? At times I think they do and at times I think they don't. If they do, it must be worse for them. They would have to fit the pad over the tip of their penis and fasten it into place with a specially devised harness. I find myself casting surreptitious looks at their crotches. I can see great unsettling bulges. Aha! I knew it all along. Men *do* have a monthly bloodlet just like us. Or maybe it's only once every three months. Or maybe when they get married it stops.

Sanitary napkins. Awful. Because we've become babies again. Just at the moment we think we've grown up, we've reverted to soiling ourselves. We have nappies pinned on us because we can't control ourselves.

And as if that's not enough, we have to tend to our little slits which have mysteriously metamorphosed from pink fuzzy apricots to dark, dank swampy holes we now call "cunts," holes that give off strange rank odours. Cheesy smells. We hope no one notices except ourselves. But they do, they do.

The boys are constantly telling jokes about the blind man and the fish shop, about Limburger cheese. We don't laugh at them anymore. Who knows if they're not referring to us when they snigger and snuffle and go on about the hundred varieties of French cheese. . . .

Sexual fantasy one: This is when the sexual fantasies begin. They amaze me. My best fantasy is about the garbage man. Our garbage man. He wears dirty frayed shorts; his thick ginger-haired legs sprout out like tree trunks. He has sun-bleached hair and nicotine-stained teeth and broad freckled hands with black-rimmed nails.

In my favourite scenario he invites me to ride in the front

of the truck with him. I'm all pink and lollypoppy and squeaky clean. My hair is curled like Shirley Temple's, and my panties have layers of coloured flounces. While he's driving, he asks me to sit on his lap. There is a lot of squeezing and pushing and breathing and jiggling up and down to the truck's rhythm. And always there is the bulge under the frayed shorts and the great soft cushion of springy ginger pubic hair. Both of us pretend that what is happening is not really happening. This is a very important part of my fantasy.

In between the jolts and jogs and grunts and groans, everybody's garbage is meticulously picked up and dumped in the back of the truck. Nobody is neglected. At the end of the rounds, Miss Frilly Pants is let out of the truck, as sweet and demure and spotless as when she first got in.

Sexual fantasy two: My second-best fantasy is about Belsen. I'm in the middle of a grey dirt compound lashed to a pole. I'm dressed like Tarzan's Jane — rags and tatters hardly conceal my budding breasts, barely cover my buttocks. Although I've been a prisoner for the duration of the war, my rosy-ripe flesh is bursting out of my rags, my skin is glowing, my eyes are bright with courage and endurance. My glossy hair swings down to my waist.

The Beast of Belsen stands over me, swastikaed, jackbooted, whip ready for another round of punishment. But I refuse to renounce my Jewishness. I refuse to renounce my nationality. I'm an Australian Jewess, proud and free — and pulsating with sex. The Beast raises his whip. I start singing "Advance Australia Fair" in Yiddish. My golden notes pour like honey over the concentration camp. Suddenly — a crack. The wooden gates with their Gothic characters *Arbeit macht frei* come toppling down. The entire gum-chewing American army stands in the compound. The men stare at me, devour me with their hungry eyes. Then a young officer — he's about fifteen — his face worn with fatigue, his clothes crumpled and stained with battle, steps forward and joins me, singing

81

in a faultless tenor. His Yiddish accent is impeccable.

> Australia's sons let us rejoice
> For we are young and free.

Mussulmen raise their typhoid-racked bodies from lice-ridden bunks; women whose wombs have been ripped from their bodies by Dr. Mengele rise from their rusty operating tables. They lift their voices in song, as do the entire liberating army. Only the curs of the SS are silent, their heads lowered in defeat and shame. My voice, like Nellie Melba's, soars above everybody else's.

——◆——

My parents were members of a committee to help war refugees. Whenever a boatload of them arrived in Sydney from that strange, unreal place called Europe, I would be taken down to the Woolloomooloo docks. "It'll be good for her to see how other Jews live. She should know what happened to us over there."

It was hard to think of those poor pathetic bodies as "us" — the women in their babushkas, the men with their foreign cloth caps and shapeless floppy trousers. And always the empty eyes staring from the wasted faces lining the boat rail.

As soon as they had filed off the gangplanks, the Jewish Welcoming Committee herded them into a large hall to feed them and reassure them as best they could that here in this strange antipodean outpost it was possible for a Jew to live a civilized life.

I used to help my mother's friends serve vegetable soup and fruit compote. It was the closest I ever came to my concentration camp fantasy. I wore white shorts which rode high over my buttocks (I always checked to make sure that my creases were showing), American Beauty halter tops and cross-over ankle-strap sandals. Carrying the bread and salt to the scarecrows at the trestle tables, I felt myself to be a combination of the Whore of Babylon and the Angel of Mercy. I was irresistible. Gaunt fifteen-year-old boys stared at me while they sucked greedily on the hot soup. They stared with envy — what lucky charm did I possess to have escaped the horrors which had overtaken them? By what accident were they sitting there, penniless and grey-faced and displaced, while I pranced around on my strong-muscled Australian legs, my face plump and smooth with ignorance.

Beneath my surface sympathy, I had nothing but a patronizing contempt for them — contempt for the boys in their ridiculous plus fours, their shabby pants hiked up to their nipple line with frayed braces; contempt for the girls of my own age who wore thick black stockings which wrinkled around their ankles and whose woollen armpits were damp with perspiration.

These were Jews? What did I have in common with them or they with me? Jewish meant spotless borders, hysterical mothers, afternoon tea tables piled high with chopped liver and *babkes*. Jewish meant dull boys with dimpled thighs and bad breath who always topped their classes, Blue Boxes in the middle of rummy tables and tea with lemon. It meant roast chicken every Saturday when the *goyim* had Sargents meat pies — or so Fanya insisted — and regular dental check-ups.

And yet I envied them. They knew something I didn't. Their unhappiness, unlike mine, was validated by the world.

—◇—

Scene: I'm parading in front of my mother's full-length pedestal mirror in my floral two-piece bathers. I step back from the mirror as far as I can, trying to see myself as passers-by would. What confronts me is a hopeless sack of potatoes with a pimply face, slug white midriff and legs which are hopelessly twisted and crooked. With such legs I shouldn't be on my way to Bondi Beach — I should be seeking admission to an orthopaedic ward. And my face! What I can see of it under the pimples, that is. My features slip and slide around my face. I'm a blob, a blot, a lump of bloated blubber. How do people recognize me when I walk down the street? They nod and smile and say "Hello, Anna," but how they manage to put this formless featureless mass together and label it correctly is beyond me. It's more than I can do. . . .

"So. Your clever friends are coming again. Your fine intelligent friends." In my mother's mouth, words like "fine," "clever," "intelligent," were transmuted into curses. "I work all week like a slave in the stinking pleating factory. *He* sits there with a book. Him and his books! Me, I have to break my back, I have to spit blood." Another of my mother's favourite activities — spitting blood. She spat enough blood in the course of an average day to flood all the spittoons of the largest TB sanatorium in Switzerland. "And now I have to shop, make food for your animals!"

"No, no, I don't want you to," I pleaded, wringing my hands. "My friends don't care if they eat. It's just that it's my turn to have them over here for an afternoon."

"My turn" came perhaps once in six weeks. Saturday afternoon meetings were held in the homes of the members of Habonim, a Zionist youth movement which I had recently joined. Its aims were to persuade young Jews to emigrate to Palestine and live on kibbutzim. I didn't need much persuading — I would have signed up to live in an igloo in Iceland if it carried with it the promise of being sprung from home.

What I loved most were the camps in which I could escape for whole weekends at a time. Plump Sydney boys and girls — myself included — were taught, along with the philosophy of Theodore Herzl, the basics of army training. Rope climbing, swimming across rivers with heavy backpacks, jumping off rooftops into precariously held sheets — all of these activities were taught with a deadly seriousness by instructors specially imported from Palestine. There wasn't one of us who didn't feel that the fate of world Jewry rested in our hands.

My favourite activity was stick fighting. A group of us would stand in a circle brandishing thick sticks. In the centre, Yossi, the instructor, barked out Hebrew commands, sprang forward and tried to crash our skulls in with his stick. I was especially good at this activity and once surpassed myself by knocking Yossi's stick clear out of the ring and taking a strip off his nose.

In what way learning how to stick fight in a Sydney suburb could help bring about a Jewish state I wasn't entirely clear, but it didn't matter. I loved the uniforms we had to wear, the earnest discussions about "self-determination," the feeling that we had set ourselves against the blandness of the happy-go-lucky Australians.

Fanya, of course, was pleased that I was being given a "Zionist education," but after a while she began to loathe the excess of zeal and lack of manners which we displayed. *Bahaimes* she called us. Wild animals. And every time it was my turn to have my group over for our meetings, she worked herself into a state of hysteria.

The food. The Food. *The Food!* Useless to protest that they didn't want the food, that *I* didn't want the food, that I'd rather she served shit on a plate as long as she served it with a smile.

"How can you invite friends unless you give them something? Who do you think I am? Because *they're* animals, *I* have to be an animal too?"

So Fanya had to prepare a table that was more elaborate, more expensive, than anyone else's. Not out of competition. That would have been too simple — even I could have dealt with that. No, it was masochism — how best to exploit the situation with a maximum of pain. At this my mother was past master.

For hours before my friends arrived Fanya ranted and raved. The whole flat had to be cleaned, borders and all. Cakes had to be baked, fancy sandwiches concocted, ice-cold drinks prepared. I bit back any protests, any remarks which might have upset her further. I was in terror that as my friends trooped up the stairs, they would hear my mother cursing.

Finally, the knock! A last pleading look at my mother. Her mouth had clamped into a hard button of disapproval; the ridge between her eyebrows had deepened. Inside the furrow I could see a line of white face powder. If only she'd stay out of sight in the kitchen. But my friends had already glimpsed my mother's hostile face. They knew what it meant. Instantly we were all on guard. We sat on our chairs, stiff with embarrassment.

Once or twice my mother passed through on her way to the bedroom. She unbuttoned her mouth, bared her teeth, buttoned up. Then the dreaded call — "Anna!" The name vibrated with tension. "Don't your friends want some little refreshment?"

No! I felt like yelling. They want you to drop dead. And I want you to drop dead too, right on the freshly waxed floor! What a refreshment *that* would be! But instead, with an apologetic half-smile, I ran out to the kitchen. My mother, the grim-faced reaper, was rigid with martyrdom.

I stumbled out and fumbled my way through the ordeal of the afternoon tea until finally it was over. Everyone was about to escape. Everyone, that is, except me. I had to clean up. My mother wouldn't hear of anyone helping me. No, that would be rude. And God forbid there should be rudeness under Fanya's gracious roof. My friends filed gratefully out of the door, their eyes moist with patronizing pity. "Anna," hissed the little black hole in the button mouth. "Anna!"

Help, Mother, what have I done? What horrible torture have I perpetrated on your exhausted hide? How many pints of blood have you spilt this time?

Balls and Books

At last. I was home free, sprung from the painful confusions of my past by a piece of paper which, miraculously, granted me entry into the magic world of University. Novels, poetry, essays. A whole world of books which, by virtue of a Commonwealth Scholarship grant, I was now actually being paid to read. I finally had a focus, a function — I was Doing Arts. . . .

But books weren't the only thing I found at university. I discovered the world of Christians, non-Jews. *Shigotsim.* Drunken *shigotsim.* They were the intellectuals, the Bohemians, the Free-Thinkers, the Libertarians. They drank, they fucked, they said things like "every act of copulation is a conscious act of opposition to the state"; they read Bertrand Russell, Havelock Ellis, and smuggled copies of *Tropic of Capricorn* and *Lady Chatterley's Lover* into Lit classes.

And they weren't Jewish. Not one of them. I'd left my Jewishness behind with my school days. My interest in Habonim deserted me the day Israel was declared a state. A nod of approval from my mother was enough to finish anything off.

University. It was perfect. The very place my father and mother made sacrifices to send me to, the place for which they did without, working their fingers to the bone to supplement my meagre scholarship money. They were now in the process of failing in a new business, a sleazy little supermarket in the Western suburbs where my mother *shlepped* the cartons and defrosted the heavy-duty freezer and did the books and scrubbed the floor; while my father, a volume of Spinoza in his hands, dozed by the cash register and allowed every hooligan to shop-lift cigarettes and bottles of beer.

Yes, university was perfect. It didn't take me more than a few days to sniff out the very group of people my parents would have hated and feared the most. And not a circumcised prick among them!

Scene: Fanya and Feivel have gone away to a country guest house for a well-earned weekend of rest. At least I hope they have and that they don't decide to come home before their time is up.

Or do I? Do I secretly long for them to return late on Saturday night and see the changes their dutiful daughter has wrought on the spotless flat with its shiny dust-free borders? Beer bottles on the carpet; the white net curtains knotted up into large ungainly lumps; ashtrays — the ones with scenes of the Wailing Wall and Hebrew University — overflowing with soggy brown roll-your-own stubs. The sofa full of fucking bodies; the bathtub full of fucking bodies; the double bed full of fucking bodies. . . .

But that's nothing. What is happening in the room with the Three Pigs curtains and the matching Three Pigs cover-let? Who is that Big Bad Wolf who is huffing and puffing and blowing their daughter — or trying to? It's Ian Crawley, a certified card-carrying Commie and an almost certified loony, that's who. In between schizophrenic bouts, he also happens to be a part-time lecturer in philosophy at Sydney University. He's skinny and pop-eyed and wears steel-rimmed spectacles which now lie on the dressing table next to a little brown money box which was given to Anna by her loving parents when she was three and which has the following cryptic legend painted on it: "Little Annale is no fool/She puts her money in her stool."

All is not lost, however. Little Annale *is* no fool. She is still "virgo intacta." She may read Sartre and Gide and know every single verse of "The Good Ship Venus"; she may allow Crawley's long white sluggy body to lie on top of her and let him stare at her already substantial boobs with his watery myopic eyes. But she won't allow his whey-coloured accordion-pleated cock to enter her hole — her holy of holies. She is keeping herself for a "meaningful experience." She's heard — and she believes — that a girl falls in love in a very special way with the man who deflowers her and remains in love with him for the rest of her life. And the idea of Ian Crawley remaining with her for even the rest of the night is more than she can bear to contemplate.

So she steadily resists Crawley's schizzy advances (afterwards she's told she's lucky he didn't pick up her money box and bash her brains out with it), and he turns aside and comes on the coverlet. Splog! Splot! Right in the eye of the second little pig, the one carrying the bundle of sticks on his back. . . . Annale's Three Pigs coverlet despoiled by the come of a lefty lunatic.

The problem is, she still feels herself an alien, an outsider. And that's a desperate feeling. To have finally found the ultimate group of outsiders and still be a stranger — that's the nightmare come true. She can't get *in*. The wild parties, the sexual permissiveness, the endless excited arguments about literature, film, politics, philosophy — she loves it, she wants passionately to be part of it, sometimes she even feels as if she *is* part of it. But she's not. She is just as much a stranger at these parties as she is at the afternoon teas with her parents' friends. At home she belongs with Them; with Them she belongs at home.

———⟨⟩———

Tom.

Tom McCarthy. The perfect first lover. Perfect because of his imperfections. "Are you sure you're doing the wrong thing?" I asked myself, and the answer with Tom was an unqualified "Yes!" Not for one moment did I delude myself into thinking that being with Tom was going to be anything but a complete disaster. The minute I laid eyes on him I knew I had found the man who would make my confused self even more confused. Here, finally, was the man to make Fanya and Feivel quake in their boots; here was the man to make Fanya and Feivel's daughter quake in her boots. I sped on towards my own unhappiness with no hesitation.

I first met Tom at a party given by Patrick Sullivan. Patrick was an architecture student, one of the few of our group who took his studies seriously. He also seemed to have money. He lived in a large glassed-in studio with a garden and threw parties every Friday night. It was, I found out later, quite by chance that Tom turned up at that particular party since he usually scorned the university crowd.

I had heard about Tom McCarthy by reputation. He was an unpublished poet, a drunkard, a self-proclaimed philosopher, a layabout who lived on handouts and the dole. "Be careful of me," were the first words Tom said to me, "I'm a wise old gypsy." I believed him, at least the parts about being old and a gypsy.

Although he was only in his early thirties, to my eighteen-year-old eyes he seemed to be a worldly-wise "older man."

While every other male in the room was so obviously a boy, Tom's shrewd caramel-coloured eyes, his splayed slippery dip of a nose, seemed to be the epitome of sophistication. The fact that his brushy moustache didn't quite manage to hide a mouthful of rotting brown stumps didn't bother me in the least. I didn't care about the stumps. What I *did* care about were the gushes of words and images which came pouring out in a never-ending stream. Bits of quotations from Oscar Wilde, Swinburne, La Rochefoucauld, Leopardi — exotic names I'd never before heard, certainly not in my literature courses. And sprinkled in between, lines from his own poetry, which even then I recognized as being weak.

A failed poet. A failed philosopher. But . . . a successful Bohemian! A brilliantly successful one. Drunk, penniless, he lived in a filthy cockroach-infested room in Newtown. His bedding was shiny and slippery as glass from lack of washing, his pillow stank, his clothes lay in infested piles on the filthy floor. No spotless borders in Tom's room. Crumbs, cigarette butts, hair balls and grease were ground into the bare planks. *Eingetroten*, as my mother would have exclaimed with disgust, if she hadn't fainted first, that is. Trodden in! Yes, Mother, it surely *was* trodden in — with what noxious effluvia, I shudder to think. But oh, Fanya, the *books*. The egg-stained, snot-flecked, dog-eared books! Books everywhere — in the sink, on the bed, in the half-open drawers, spilling off the rickety shelves, all over the floor — *eingetroten* over the entire room. Nietzsche, Schopenhauer, Dostoevsky, Kafka, Rimbaud. Chaotic nightmare visions. Apocalyptic thunderings from the Great Madhouse in the Sky. This was life. This, finally, was what it was all about. Not the well-behaved maunderings of the gentlefolk at the university; the discreet rustle of lecture notes, the chalk dust lying thick in the air. Here is where it all was, right here in this very room where the dark underbelly of Europe's culture lay outstretched before me on the splintery floorboards of Tom's sleazy bedsit . . . and where Anna will stretch herself out on the lumpy mattress there to surrender her closely guarded virginity. . . .

Re-enter Miss Frilly Pants. Re-enter the Garbage Man. But it's a good many years on now and the Garbage Man *reads*! He has a big library and a big prick. Balls and books. The perfect combination. There's only one thing missing. Or rather not missing. Miss Frilly Pants is a virgin. An unwilling virgin. She's been keeping herself all this time for Mr. Wrong. And she's found him. . . .

Scene: Miss Frilly Pants has disappeared forever. A miracle has been performed. An unbelievably huge shaft of skin and blood vessels — "engorged with blood" as they say in the sex manuals — has disappeared up a microscopic hole, that same hole where not too long ago fat Carlton couldn't even insert a twig. A reverse birth, where instead of an immensity forcing its way out of a minuteness, the reverse has occurred. The nightmare hallucinations of her childhood are righted. Balance has been restored. The huge pencil has finally scrawled its message on the minuscule sheet of paper; the giant billiard ball has dropped neatly into the dwarf-sized pocket.

She is pinned against the stained sheets; he, Ubermensch, is lying sweating on top of her. If she moves her head very carefully to one side she can see a well-thumbed copy of *Thus Spake Zarathustra* on the floor. This, she thinks, is what life is all about, and by some grace, some miracle, she has been lucky enough to find it.

I'm *doing* it!

I'm doing it!

I'm doing *it*!

Now when I go into buses and trams I don't just wonder who's menstruating — I wonder who has just finished fucking. Or who is on her way to be fucked. Or even more daring — who has been menstruating and fucking all at the same time. I'm an enthusiastic week-old fuckee.

I run from Tom's slippery grey sheets to my crisp Reckitt's Blue ones. From Baudelaire to the Three Pigs. I've insisted on reclaiming my own bedroom. I can no longer bear my mother's obscene hostile body warmth. The double bed has been sawn in half and my parents again share, if not a bed, if not a life, then at least a room. Like the double bed, I too feel as if I've been sawn in half. My two lives are drifting apart and I'm powerless to stop the drift. I've cut off all relationships with the "good girls" and the "nice boys" of my parents' circle. I am the Black Sheep. I am the Scarlet Woman. Drifting in limbo. Lost. Floating. . . .

The decayed old tenement house where Tom had a room served as home for a hard core of about ten regulars and a doss house for a floating population of hundreds. The focus of the house, the hard gem-like flame around which all others fluttered like so many devoted moths, was Archie Atkins, self-styled guru of the western world. He was the Chosen One, sent from the Old World to bring the Word to the New, which presumably had not yet become too jaded with a surfeit of such prophets. The fact that Archie was a Borstal boy didn't detract for one moment from his image. On the contrary. We never tired of hearing about Archie's poverty-stricken life in London's East End, where his mother, convinced she had given birth to the Messiah, washed his feet every day with her hair. Clearly, no one except her son had shared her vision, and after some misdemeanour, he was shipped off, like convicts of old, to the outer darkness of the colonies.

The excitement of it! Archie sitting at the kitchen table, his acolytes around him, preaching the gospel of Anarcho-Technocracy — the supremacy of infallible machines over fallible humans. The kitchen, with all the paraphernalia of Bohemia, was like a bad set from a minor Italian opera — a splintery table with half-finished bottles of cheap wine, cracked plates with the dried-out remnants of spaghetti, old Chianti bottles splotched with the bulbous growths of burnt-out candles. The electricity had long since been cut off for non-payment of bills, so Archie had simply punched holes in the rotting walls where the gas pipes were located and put a match to the escaping gas. All night and all day, in the heat of summer, the blue flames would jet out from three or four points in the peeling wall, illuminating the planes of Archie's face as he sat preaching to his underground coven. The fact that these daringly wild ideas were half-digested Marinetti, half-baked Nietzsche, didn't bother any of us.

Archie's obsessions became our obsessions. "Power over things!" he would shout, and thump the table till the wine jiggled in the empty jam jars which served as glasses. His eyes would glare with a maniacal energy, his lank black hair fall across his pallid brow, his frail body pulsate with passion.

I was fascinated by him, but in spite of his hypnotic rhetoric, his zany Cockney wit, there was never the slightest quiver of sexual attraction. I wanted to be, not his lover but his disciple. It was far more exciting than being the disciple of some timid philosophy professor, his shanks falling away to little bits of knotted muscle inside his baggy corduroys. University, I had come to realize, was just an extension of life at home. An Anglo-Saxon version, true — and that was worth a frisson or two — but otherwise just as predictable, just as proscriptive.

In Archie's kitchen lay danger, brilliance, true subversiveness. Here was someone to fill the gaps, to give my amorphous anger and unhappiness a focus. It was the world which was imperfect, not me. The emptiness belonged out there, among the Philistines.

A Penis Has No Nose

Scene: "I'm going to kiss you all over," says Tom. He announces it with an earnest significance and looks at me carefully to watch my reaction. There is none. Why should "kiss all over" elicit any reaction from a woman who has been relieved of the twenty-ton burden of her virginity and who is flying high? So Tom kisses my forehead. He kisses my nose and my mouth and my neck and my breasts and my rib cage and my navel and my stomach — and I'm expecting him to kiss my thighs and my knees and my feet and my toes. But he's stopped at something on the way. He has stopped *there*! I'm flabbergasted. Unbelieving. Surely he has made a mistake. A gauche embarrassing mistake. Surely he couldn't want to kiss *that*! The place which I've touched only with the greatest trepidation, the place which I bandage with the tenderest care every month. The place which I've never in my entire life even looked at. If he succeeds in opening my legs, he's going to see it! I want him to stop. This has nothing to do with fucking — a penis has no nose, it has no eyes. Compared to what this man is now intent on doing, fucking's almost impersonal. But this! Unthinkable. I try to pull his head higher up. I try to push his head lower down. But no — his great bullet of a head is unshiftable. And he's forcing my legs open. Gently — but forcing. And suddenly he's there. Right in the middle of that moist jungly swamp. His whole face. His mouth. His tongue. The sensation's unbearable. What's happening to me? I'm diminishing in size. I'm shrinking. And my cunt is swelling, swelling. Taking me over. I'm disappearing up my own hole, racing towards a place I've never before visited. I dig my fingers into Tom's head, jamming it up tight against me. There is a split second of "hold" and in that second a faraway voice tells me that I'm going to let go and pee all over Tom's face. All over the face of a stranger. I'm scared and ashamed. And then wave after wave comes crashing down and I don't give a damn. I'm drowning. He's drowning. The room's drowning. . . .

Scene: I tell my parents I'll be going to a film at the University Film Society so it will hardly be worthwhile, will it, to drag all the way home after my late-afternoon lectures. I'll grab a bite at the Students' Union and then go on to the film . . . blah . . . blah . . . blah. . . .

I'm trembling and tense with the effort of lying, of keeping up appearances. But I needn't worry that my parents will suspect a larger crime behind the smaller one that I'm fobbing off on them — what I'm telling them is tragedy enough. My "Zionist animals" have now metamorphosed for my mother into my "University low lives." That includes anyone who isn't a member of the Jewish Students' Union, like all the good little daughters of her friends. Like all the good little sons, too, who look as if they've had one suck too many at their mummies' titties — if I look carefully I can see faint bubbles of breast milk in the corners of their mouths.

Film societies. Drama groups. *"Dreck!"* says my father who, when the crunch comes, forsakes his silence and closes rank with the Great Washed. *"Goyishe dreck!"*

98

"A film society evening," mocks Fanya. "For her, for my darling daughter, all of a sudden Hoyts isn't good enough. For Esther it's good enough. For Ruthie it's good enough. But for my precious daughter, nothing is good enough. Art films she needs. Her and her low lives. Her and her anti-Semites. Her pogromniks."

Oh, Fanya. If you react like this because you're taken in by my feeble lie about going to a film, what would you say if I told you that I was going across the city to a tenement house? That I was going to take off my clothes, lie down in a filthy stained bed, open my legs and allow an anti-Semitic drunkard to roll his *traife* wine-stained tongue around my kosher clitoris. And when I'd had enough of that — greedy, lustful traitor to my race that I am — I will bend over and take into my mouth, not your Lady Macbeth tit, Fanya, that squirted gall into my hungry mouth, but a huge uncircumcised cock which will give me more milky nourishment than you ever did. Slurp, slurp. Swallow, swallow. Yummy, Mummy. . . .

Scene: If I open my eyes, I'm going to get a handful of crushed light bulb ground into them. I'm sitting bare-arsed on a splintery wooden floor, my back jammed up against a rusting iron bedstead. Tom is kneeling in front of me, naked. In his bleeding right hand is a Mazda light bulb which he has crushed into fragments. He holds his fist about half an inch from my face. All I need to trigger that menacing fist into action is to open my eyes, make a murmur, move my head.

I wait, frozen. Tom is breathing a sickly sour wino breath all over me. "You cunt. You middle-class Jewish cunt. I'll send you back to your Bellevue Hill shithouse with ground glass up your bourgeois cunt. What's left over, that is, after

I've ground your shithouse face into it."

I know enough by now to shut my mouth, to shut my ears, to shut my eyes. This isn't happening to me. It's happening to someone else, some stranger. If I try hard I can remove myself from where I am. I can shift back into the day, into the morning, where I'm eating cornflakes in Bellevue Hill, drinking orange juice, brushing my teeth with Kolynos, washing my school-girl complexion with Palmolive. I know that if I will myself out of existence on this small space of floor, Tom will withdraw his fist, let the splinters of glass fall to the ground, let me escape. Yet again. . . .

Variation one: My head is pulled back taut over a rickety banister, a fistful of my hair in one of Tom's hands, in the other the jagged end of a broken beer bottle. "Hello, darling," says Tom and starts making sawing motions with the bottle so close to my throat I can feel it tickle. . . .

Variation two: It is nearly 12:30. I have to be home by 12:59 at the latest. As long as one can say the magic figure "12" then somehow it's moral, safe, in the grassy-green realm of the permissible. After that, it's the desert land of A.M. where virgin princesses turn into tattered trollops, and Jewish princes into pagan frogs. Tom knows this, and uses his knowledge. It's an ugly game he plays with me.

"It's 12:30," he says, concern in his voice. "Isn't it time you started home if you don't want to get into trouble?"

As always, I'm caught in the apparent innocence of his remark; and this time, like all others, I must pay the price for my stupid naivete. I reach for my clothes, put on my jacket, make it to the front door, turn the knob, manage to get a foot out onto the street.

Tom pounces on me. The cat has caught the mouse. "You didn't really think I would let you go, did you, little bourgeois cunt? Can't wait to get back to your cozy little bedroom. Can't wait to be a good little girl again for your mummy and daddy."

And the countdown begins. The waiting game. Twelve-thirty. One o'clock. One-thirty. . . . I sit in a corner. Tom weaves around the room glugging down pints of cheap plonk. By now he's thoroughly drunk. Sozzled. And nasty as hell. Finally he tires of his own malevolence and lets me go — I think. I can never be sure. Tentatively I turn the doorknob, step outside. I try to walk as slowly and as calmly as I can. Once when I made the fatal mistake of running, Tom closed in on me like a flash. It cost me an extra hour. The further I get from the front door, the faster I walk. Finally, I'm running. I've escaped. From what, I'm not too sure. To what I have no idea. But now — right now — I'm safe. Until next time. . . .

Obvious question one: Why does there have to be a next time?

Answer: Because I've become a sex addict, a sex junkie. Whenever I arrive home after a shattering experience with Tom — and they've now become routine — I swear I'll never see him again. The equation has become quite clear in my head — fucking him means being tortured by him. If I forego the fucking I forego the inevitable sadism afterwards. If I put myself in his power one way, I also have to submit to his power in other ways. I resolve never to have anything to do with him again and to go out with Patrick Sullivan who has been calling me. Patrick is attractive and bright and funny. I like him a lot. But I know it won't work. He's intent on becoming an architect. How can I go to bed with a man who is passionate about building things on the ground out of bricks and cement? Tom may be a loser, but he builds castles in the air.

The week wears on and I wear down. I can't concentrate on lectures. All I can concentrate on is a hot throbbing between my legs, a wetness, a swollen tightness. I slaver.

Literally. Like Moses' pillar of flame, Tom's prick rises up in front of me. Like Moses I have no choice but to follow it. I chase it across the city. It's true, after all, what they say about virgins and their deflowerers. Phone calls. Taxis. Once when I had no money left, I walked five miles just so I could stretch out on that creaking iron bedstead.

Tom knew the power he had over me. He also knew that the moment I had satisfied myself, I wanted out. It was this he could never forgive in me. A desperate man, it made him even more desperate and violent.

Obvious question two: Why didn't I leave Fanya and Feivel and set up my own place as so many of my friends were doing?

Answer: Because I felt just as alienated from my "low lives" as I did from my family. Because I didn't exist, and to move from a despised known to a threatening unknown would have obliterated me completely. Rule — if you don't exist, then stay at home where at least the pretence of existence can be kept up. After all, you've been doing it for so long, you're bound to have developed some sort of lopsided skill at it.

So the risky game of nerves continued. The two parts that never connected. In one incarnation I took the 333 bus from Bellevue Hill to Eddy Avenue and then a tram to Addison Road. Only forty minutes stood between one part of my unhappy life with my parents, and the other part of my unhappy life with Tom, but the difference was cataclysmic — the bus might just as well have been a time-travel capsule transporting me from one galaxy to another.

In the other incarnation I attended the engagement parties of my childhood friends in the ballroom of the Chevron, wearing an off-the-shoulder ice-blue net confection; my parents smiling through clenched teeth at another family's *nachas* which for some unfathomable reason their daughter denied them. Out of spite, they believed. And perhaps in their unwitting way they were right. Perhaps it *was* done out of spite. Perhaps my whole life was lived out of spite and that's why it had never belonged to me. . . .

Tom's drunkenness, his loutish brutality, his insidious weakness, made me despise him, even as I desired him. I wanted him to disappear in a puff of smoke, leaving only Archie Atkins and the excitement of the kitchen-table anarchists. But I couldn't have one without the other. I was so frightened of Tom that, ironically, home had turned into a haven, into the very place I longed for it to be when I was a child.

That frightening jungle where fathers and daughters performed Acts of Darkness, where hateful and puzzling battles were fought out amongst three savage antagonists — this was now, by a wave of Tom's avenging prick, transformed into a snug suburban nest where gas fires hissed comfortingly against blustery Sydney nights, where Dick Fair's "Amateur Hour" held sway on the radio every Thursday night between 8:00 and 9:00, and where a phone call after 9:30 was considered a death knell to civilized living.

This was the place where at the flick of a wireless dial, Mary Livingstone, M.D. stepped into your life to remind you that every cloud had a silver lining; where that kindly old pragmatist, Dr. Mac, healed the troubles of the universe; and where First Light Frazer single-handedly outwitted the entire German army. In this warm cozy world, Mrs. 'Obbs nattered endlessly to Mrs. Bottomley over the back fence, Aeroplane Jelly flew high, and the world's illnesses could be cured by Bonnington's Irish Moss Gum Jubes made of petrol oxymel of carrageen found off the coast of Ireland.

Home had finally achieved the sort of peace I had always imagined other lucky children enjoyed. Except that I was no longer a child. I was some sort of hybrid.

The yo-yo kept jerking up and down but the bounce was rapidly wearing out. I couldn't keep up the double life. The strain of deception was too great, Sydney too small. . . .

Fanya sensed that I was slipping from her grasp. The borders could no longer contain me. Now none of my friends came to the flat, neither the "wild animals" who had long since been discarded, nor my newfound "low lives" from the university. There was no enemy left to attack — not even me — or if there was, it was lurking far beyond her reach.

Feivel too retreated even further from my life. We hardly saw one another, even though we were sharing the same living space. Once when I arrived home at 2:30 A.M. I bumped into him coming out of the bathroom. Tom had given me a bad time and my face was tear streaked. In my hand I clutched a crumpled bra. My father's eyes dropped from my face to the bra. He stared at it. Then, without saying a word, he shuffled back into the bedroom.

Scene: I'm going out to have an all-day study session with a girl friend, I tell Fanya. She lives so far away I'll have to leave home at 7:30 in the morning without having breakfast. In reality, I sneak across the road to have an abortion. The abortion clinic is on Bellevue Road, Bellevue Hill. That's right. It is directly across the road from our block of flats. In a white stucco villa-type house which has Seaview Rest Home printed discreetly in gold lettering on the mailbox.

This innocent-looking building that I pass every day — an abortion mill? The mind boggles. Do the sadistic nurses buy their afternoon tea cakes at Baum's Continental Pastries? Do the evil doctors who each day break the Hippocratic oath munch, in between "scrapes," apples bought at Donato's Fresh Fruit and Veg? Is the clinic supplied with gauzes and sanitary pads and antiseptics from Richard Wren, Chemist? Do the local garbage men who pick up *our* respectable refuse — chicken bones, fruit skins, egg shells, tea leaves — also empty bins from the Seaview Rest Home full of half-formed foetuses, great bloody chunks of afterbirths, a wispy hank of hair, maybe even a tiny shell-pink fingernail?

So many times I've pretended to my parents that I'm "just going around the corner," and then scooted halfway across the city for a quick hot fuck. Now I'm pretending to go out of town to study with a friend, but I'm just sneaking across the road, a box of sanitary pads in one hand, a briefcase full of camouflaging Eng. Lit. textbooks in the other. A quick look up and down Bellevue Road, a furtive dash across the street, a guilty knock at the front door. And then I'm in a hospital bed wearing a patched smock and looking out across the street to see my mother straightening the curtains of our living room.

Like Scylla and Charybdis, the two jagged rocks of my life are threatening to clash together, with me crushed to smithereens in between. Torn-off pieces of my hospital smock are tossed into the air by the grey swirling foam. . . .

A furtive pass of an envelope containing 75 pounds quickly belies the carefully nurtured illusion that this is a respectable and benevolent nursing home for upper-income geriatrics. I'm hauled onto a stretcher for a dizzying ride down the corridors. Jesus, give me a mask or something to cover my face! What if I see Mrs. Weiss, my mother's close friend, being wheeled back from the opposite direction? If I'm having an "illegal operation" less than a hundred yards from where my mother is fiddling with the parlour curtains, anything is possible. . . .

Dr. Mephisto, with his white mask and his criminal scalpel, bends over me and says in a patronizing mock-jovial tone, "How are we doing, Mrs. Jones?"

"I'm not Mrs. Jones, you schmuck, and you know it!" I manage to spit out before having my legs hoisted up and fastened with leather straps to two icy-cold metal stirrups.

Since this is a high-class outfit, there's a woman in white assisting at the operation. She's wearing a nursing sister's veil. Crisp, efficient, respectable. But it's all so sinister — like a nightmare fancy-dress party where Ilse Koch comes dressed up as Florence Nightingale. Who are they supposed to be fooling? Well, maybe a Mrs. Weiss would allow herself to be fooled, but not me. I know exactly why I'm here and what's happening. And it's awful. Grotesque. A grotesque inverted parody of the sexual act — I lie on my back, my legs are apart, a man is between them. Something hard is being inserted. I moan.

But everything is anti-sex. I can feel my vagina being forced wide open by calipers, a cold metal hardness being pushed against my uterus. A silver-steel feel-up. And then the thin, cruel probe. "Relax, Mrs. Jones."

Yes, I'm relaxing. It's okay. It's okay. The beginning of a familiar dull period pain. But it grows thinner, edgier, sharper. The pain steepens. Get out of there, you sadistic bastard. *Get out of there.*

Frau Koch puts her hand out to steady me. I sink my teeth into it and she jumps away from the table and turns her back to me.

I'll never make love again as long as I live. I don't want anybody or anything inside me, ever. Just get out. Leave me alone. I hate your bleary blue eyes staring up at me above your surgical mask. I hate the drops of sweat on your oily forehead. I hate your hands pushing and probing and stabbing at my vulnerable soft insides.

And then — merciful relief. I'm still surging with pain but it's my pain now. No foreign bodies inside me. No enemy aliens. The joy, the relief of the return journey. A cup of tea, a couple of aspirin, an antibiotic pill administered to me by Ilse Nightingale. I've bitten the hand that feeds me — dare I trust her? But I realize I'm anonymous to her, a neutral blank, someone for whom it's not even worth expending the energy of feeling resentful or angry.

Tom calls for me. But I can't go home yet. It's too early. I have to wait until dinner time or else my going-out-of-town-for-the-day alibi won't hold up. Will he, diabolically, insist this time that I go home early? But no — he's sober and contrite and male-guilty. In a spasm of responsibility, he's even collected the 75 pounds from the dosshouse residents. He's had his pleasure — I've copped the pain. The old time-honoured story. But it's too hoary even for me to buy, so I comfort him. I'm so relieved he isn't drunk and belligerent that I'll do anything.

When it's sufficiently dark I hobble out of the front door on Tom's arm, the sanitary napkin feeling like a Brillo pad against my shaved pubis. Again I'm struck by the grotesqueness of it all. We're like a parody of a maternity hospital exit — "Just Tommy and me/And Baby makes three." Except I'm not carrying a bundle of joy in my arms. I'm clutching at my box of pads and the counterfeit bundle of books.

Back home in time for dinner. How is it possible that Fanya doesn't know, that she can't see it written all over my face? Doesn't she smell the pungent odour of antiseptic which hangs around me? Can't she twig to the fact that I'm having my period at a strange time of the month? What if I forget to lock the bathroom door and she comes in and notices my pubic hair has all been shaved off? "Hello, Fanya, how do you like my mons veneris today? It's the latest fashion. . . . "

I'm sweating with tension. I sense something ominous in Fanya's silence, in the almost wilful blankness of her eyes. But she notices nothing — or decides to notice nothing.

—◇—

For the next couple of weeks I was more at peace than I had been for years. Tom was still suffering from guilt which I didn't try to talk him out of; on the contrary, I did all I could to maintain it. Lust left me strictly alone. And my mother, sensing a momentary weakness in me, softened. Life limped on. . . .

The abortion marked a turning point. I was unpregnant. Reborn. I had to have more space. The walls were closing in on me; not even the entire continent of Australia was large enough. I had, by some miracle, earned my BA. It was the lowest pass anyone could get without failing, but I was amazed to be given any official recognition at all. And Grandfather Zuckerman had left me a small legacy, along with his fob watch. It wasn't much but it was enough for a one-way ticket out of Australia.

But where to go? The last place in the world I wanted to live in was London, the lodestar which beckoned every Australian. I could have gone there to teach tax-free. I could have tried some free-lance writing — everybody knew that Fleet Street lived off the genius of Australian journalists. But somehow England was an anathema to me. It was Australia writ large. "Home," as the Australians put it. No. I wanted to go to America, the place where I should have been born, where my parents should have gone in the first place. Where all European Jews should have gone. But America was out. I couldn't work there. Instead, I had to settle for Canada. Montreal. Although some of Feivel's relatives lived there, it was at least close to New York.

Across a Cardboard Sea

I no longer had to stare in the window of the P and O Line in Circular Quay at the perfect replica of a liner with tiny portholes and matchstick railings and wisps of cotton-wool smoke coming from its funnels as it steamed its way across a cardboard sea. I held in the zip pocket of my wallet a piece of paper which entitled me to a space of my own behind one of those portholes. I was now a member of that privileged cabal — an Overseas Traveller.

I had anticipated the most terrible scenes from Fanya when she finally realized that I was serious about leaving, but she was curiously subdued. "Nu," she said to me, "maybe in Canada you'll settle down and stop your running around with the crazies. Maybe there you'll come to your senses. You'll realize maybe that your parents can't be so terrible after all. *Efshe* . . . maybe. . . "

I sensed in her a feeling of relief. She would be spared further embarrassment from a daughter who not only hadn't had an engagement party at the Chevron but who openly scoffed and scorned those steady boys — the ones who were left over, that is, from the first frantic picking of the pink-tulled girls. For the dread phrase "on the shelf," she could now substitute the semi-respectable "going overseas." At least it enabled my parents to murmur something in self-defence when they were quizzed by concerned friends in between rummy games.

Fanya and Feivel, sensing that they were about to be left alone together, had made a sort of truce. Just about a month before I was to sail, Feivel brought home a budgie in a cage, the first pet that had ever been introduced into our household. "Get it away!" shouted Fanya. "*Feh!* There'll be fleas everywhere. Bird *dreck* all over the cage! Get that *shmutz* out of here!"

But my father, on one of those rare occasions when he fixed on a course of action, refused to give way. He wanted the bird to stay. Within a few days, Fanya was completely won over. "Toshy" she called the tiny budgie, and it brought out a streak of maternal tenderness in her which I had never enjoyed. Every morning Toshy was let out of his cage and allowed to fly around the kitchen where he would perch on my father's hand and peck at a rusk offered him by Fanya.

The perfect family. Sometimes, looking at the three of them together, I would experience a sharp stab of pain. Could it have been jealousy?

I didn't dare tell Tom I was leaving. He would have finished me off for sure if he had found out that this time, when I skipped out on him, I wouldn't return. I had recurring nightmares in which he accepted, with a seemingly gentle calm, the news of my going. In my dreams, he came down to the dock to see me off and threw me a coloured streamer. I leaned over the rails to catch it, and as the ship moved out to the strains of the "Maoris' Lament" I could feel the streamer grow taut between us. But unlike the others, it didn't snap. Increasing distance only made it stronger, and try as I might, I couldn't loosen it from my clenched fist. It pulled me over the rail, dragged me through the choppy water and delivered me, sodden and freezing, at Tom's feet. "You didn't think I'd let you go, did you, little bourgeois cunt?" said Tom softly as he smiled down at me with great sweetness.

I didn't tell any of my friends that I was going, for fear they'd spill the beans to Tom. But he sniffed out my nervousness and became more and more abusive. He sensed I was planning to escape.

The night before my ship was to sail, Tom called up the flat. It was the one taboo he had never broken. He knew that invading my life at home would mean the end of our affair.

Fanya answered in the refined tone she had adopted for the phone. I could hear a high-pitched blur of sound out of which the word "fuck" leapt from time to time. Fanya held onto the phone for a minute or two. Then she banged it down. "Hoodlum!" she said in disgust. "Some filthy *shicker* low-life hoodlum!" And she gave me a long, hard stare.

The ship was to sail at 4:00 P.M. My cabin was crowded with members of my family. The ship's photographer arranged us into posed groups.

"If any man can show any just cause why this ship and this woman may not lawfully be joined together in holy departure let him now speak or else hereafter forever hold his peace," intones the ship's captain.

"I can!" bellows a wild drunken Tom, leaping into the middle of the carefully arranged photographer's tableau.

But click, click, the photo was taken and there was no devil in sight. Only Fanya and Feivel, and the rest of the family, including two lucky "little nippers" who had finally been born to Jack and Bashka. And me, cute as a button in a light-grey suit, cream blouse, orange beret perched jauntily on my Veronica Lake hair. Even little orange shorty gloves with which to let my coloured streamers trail into the Pacific as the ship pulled further and further from that dangerous shore.

"Now is the hour when we must say Good-byyyyye. . . . "

The shore line recedes. The faces blur. I'm free. No longer my parents' child, no longer my country's charge. I'm going away to where the glass eye of my great-grandmother can no longer find me.

Part II

Alice Through the Looking Glass

Montreal was empty. All I could see when I ventured out onto the street were vast tundras of snow where crow-like figures of nuns and priests were silhouetted across an iron-grey sky. And all I could hear were the hushed swish of cars and the muffled footsteps of the occasional pedestrian hurrying the devil knew where in this city. Montreal — closed, unyielding, hostile, secretive. A city held in the clenched fist of winter. A city? No — a village, and a distinctly uncharming one at that, with half the population — the French part — living on one side of the dividing line, Bleury Avenue, and the English part living on the other. Bleury. Bleuw-rr-y. A name that sounded like a particularly revolting belch.

And who were these Frenchies anyway? My entire knowledge of them was confined to a single childhood viewing of *The Country Doctor*. But what connection did bluff hearty Papa Dionne and his five adorable curly-headed moppets have with these pale, pimpled, undernourished faces, the faces of losers? The women with their ill-fitting dentures and the men with their mean little toothbrush moustaches. And what did the harsh sounds of their patois have in common with the refined cadences of the French I'd been taught at Sydney's Alliance Française?

What, for that matter, did any of Canada have in common with my images of it? Where were those intrepid settlers whose children were snatched from them in the dead of night by redskin savages, just as Captain Marryat had described it? Or those muscley Mounties clad in skin-tight jodhpurs who sang stirring songs of romance and adventure as they galloped through acres and acres of pine forests? And where, oh where, were those "Men of the Frozen North" who, according to Australian radio commercials, took giant swigs of Buckley's Canadiol Mixture to ease their hacking coughs, accompanied by background sounds of baying wolves, howling winds and yapping huskies?

My parents had written to my aunts and uncles in Montreal to let them know I was arriving and to ask them to keep an eye on me. I was to stay with my father's older sister, Bronya, until I could take care of myself. Since I had only enough money to last for a month, I submitted to my Aunty Bronya's orders and used her place as a base.

Feivel's family — *my* family, as I had to remind myself — did not match my picture of them. Where were the large cars, the gleaming modern appliances, the deep-pile carpets? Compared to Aunty Bronya's apartment on St. Urbain Street, our Bellevue Hill flat was a palace of light and luxury. It was true that Archie and Tom and my old Sydney friends lived in run-down places, but they were romantic hideaways full of books and candles and bamboo and cushions on the floor. They were not poor — they just didn't have money.

But *this* — this was poor. The outdoor staircases which leaned drunkenly against the tenement buildings in that cold, dreary snow-filled street; the ridiculous length of string which, when jerked from Bronya's second-floor flat, snapped open the front-door latch; the stuffy overheated rooms filled with threadbare carpeting, and the shabby furniture covered with cheap crackling plastic.

This was North America? Were these my prosperous overseas relatives — these outlandish "Yiddy" Jews with their singsong accents, their dark, heavy clothing, their strange yet slightly familiar features? They were all assembled in Bronya and Hershy's kitchen — aunts, uncles and cousins who reminded me of those refugees who shuffled down the gangplanks in the docks of Sydney, fresh from a Europe which was as strange to me as Australia was to them.

They had all come to greet me — Anna, the prodigal daughter of the prodigal brother who had wound up, by some quirk of Jewish fate, in the barbarian land of "Ostralya." They spoke of my father in hushed, reverential tones, handing me faded dog-eared family photos and asking me to identify which of the serious young men posing in formal groups was my father. One of the photos they showed me was of my grandmother in her coffin surrounded by her small suffering sons. It gave me a pang to see such a familiar object of my childhood in these foreign surroundings.

Soon after my arrival, my Canadian cousins — prodded by the bossy Bronya, who was acting out of a fierce family loyalty — tried to "fix me up." No matter how much I protested, they were convinced that I had come to Montreal for only one reason — to find a husband.

I was now subjected to a barrage of blind dates. The blind feeling up the blind. These Montreal boys were the clones of the Sydney ones, and I grew to dread those awkward silences which fell between us as soon as we were led into one another's presence, that thick hopeless thud when we realized that we were doomed to spend an entire evening together.

I was desperate to move out of the suffocating atmosphere of Bronya's apartment, desperate to find a job which would give me the necessary funds to start a life of my own. Since it was mid-winter, it was impossible to find a job teaching in a private school, something which I had been told was relatively easy to obtain. I put in my applications for the autumn term (doctoring them up with evidence of much teaching experience) and, in the meantime, got a job as an assistant in a downtown bookstore. It paid badly but at least it helped to restore some kind of balance to the shaky sense of myself. Ah, the solid comfort of books, the familiar reassurance of words. Every morning when I came in, I sucked in a deep breath of their pulpy paper comfort and knew, with a sense of relief, that I'd be able to get through the day.

With my first paycheque I moved out of St. Urbain Street to a small cheaply furnished basement apartment on Shuter Street. My relatives were appalled. Yes, they understood that I wanted to be independent, but to them independence was a rented room in the home of a nice Jewish family in Snowdon. A *shmootsig* apartment downtown? Who needed it? Who wanted it? Me. I did. And for the first time in my life I was able to have it.

Not that I myself didn't entertain severe doubts about my new home. When I stepped inside the front door with my two suitcases and surveyed my newly acquired territory, I howled. The snow was piled high above the small mean windows which were set flush with the ground and let in a minimal amount of light. The radiators hissed and gurgled and emitted a fierce dry heat which sandpapered my itching skin and made the inside of my skull feel like a tinderbox.

An unexpected wave of homesickness swamped me. I pined for the sappy smells of Sydney, the brilliance of the colours, the salty breezes. I even discovered to my horror that I didn't know how to take care of myself, that I was as dependent on bourgeois comforts as the most despised offspring of my mother's friends. For weeks I recycled my laundry and lived off pizzas, cokes and doughnuts.

In a panic I set to work to recreate the atmosphere of those envied rooms of my Sydney friends. I discarded the framework of the bed and set the mattress on the floor, threw a coloured scarf over the ugly lamp shade, stuck a coloured candle into a wine bottle and purchased an Indian spread to throw over the sagging sofa. But it wasn't enough.

I existed in a vacuum. I needed to be invented; otherwise

my outer covering would dissolve, my ectoplasm float in grey frozen wisps out of the window over the indifferent Canadian landscape. . . .

Until Alex Jacobs came into the bookstore one day and saved me from dissolution. Alex Jacobs. The one writer I had heard of since arriving in Canada, the one name which seemed to have any wild poetic resonance in this most prosy land. Alex's three books were on the shelf in the back of the store in a section labelled "Canadian Literature." Since the term "Australian Literature" would have sounded ludicrous in my ears — had I even heard of it — "Canadian Literature" sounded even more so. And the scrawny thin-blooded books did little to dispel my impression. They looked as if they were apologizing for their own existence. All except those of Alex Jacobs. Although they were just as scrawny-looking as the rest, there was something about them — a brash cheekiness, an arrogant self-assertion — which made them look as if they were about to leap off the shelf.

And now here he was himself, barrelling through the store, arms churning like a swimmer. The air parted in front of him like the Red Sea.

"Nietzsche!" he yelled. "Give me Nietzsche! You can throw away all your other books. Except mine of course."

Blue eyes blazing, black hair flying, body spilling over with energy — there was a magnetism about Alex Jacobs into which I was drawn from the limbo of outer space.

With you, Alex, I was finally in. I was Alice through the Looking Glass yanked through that tantalizing watery scrim which separated mundane reality from the enchanted world of fantasy. I touched your hand and suddenly I was through, leaving behind on that other sordid side the entrails of my great-grandmother, the bloody sponge of my grandfather's hemorrhaged tissues, the sad defeat of my father's blue-white cock. You were the Omphalus. No, you were more. You were both the world and its navel. I wanted to dive through your belly button until I disappeared, all except for one eye which would peer out at the world through its warm hairy peephole. All snug and safe and hidden and rooted in my secret cubbyhole.

Alex Jacobs. The Poet. The Genius. The man who was there — solid and sure and round and contained. You fed into all my needs. You were the daddy I could fuck without guilt; the lover I could fuck without fear. I had to have you. No, I had to have you have me. That would prove my existence beyond all doubt. The final proof. The final solution. There was a marvellous inevitability to it all.

We looked into each other's eyes — and saw ourselves. We looked like each other. We *were* each other. Alex was me with hair on my chest, with bunchy muscles on my arms, with thick, black hair sprouting from my scalp. A strong unconquerable me. The mirror had always betrayed me; but looking into the mirror of Alex's eyes, I saw for the first time a reflection which was real, which had definition. I was no longer an amorphous blob whose centre didn't hold. My mirror image was more me than I was myself. Along with this revelation came the instant terrible fear — if Alex looked away for even one second or closed his eyes or refused, for whatever reason, to fix his sight upon me, then my sparrow-self would fall to earth dead, lying there to await the resurrection of his gaze.

And Alex, looking into the mirror of me, knew that he had found his True Believer, one whose faith would never waver because if the Believer lost her faith, she lost her self.

This we knew, although we didn't know we knew. Our needs, like two odd jagged pieces of jigsaw, flew across the bookstore and slotted tightly together. It was a perfect fit. So perfect that neither of us bothered to stand back and take note of the fact that the pattern we made was all wrong.

Fellow Fanatics

Scene: I'm ecstatic. It's Alex's day off from the university where he teaches part-time and he's asked me to go for a car ride in the country. *Un jour à la campagne.* Except that here in this strange awful landscape the country is a place to be avoided, ignored. Spending a day in it means — at least to Alex — driving through miles and miles of dangerously slippery roads and finally stalling in a snowbank at the end of nowhere.

Ill-starred lovers that we are, we have to make a life-and-death decision — do we turn off the motor and freeze to death, or do we leave it running and risk carbon monoxide poisoning? We opt for the former. We don't need artificial heat — Alex will warm us with a recital of his latest poems. I'm excited. It's here again. Literature. This writing life. The only one I can hook into and onto. Alex declaims passionately, his eyes lifting from his page to my face, linking us, knotting us together in a holy trinity — him, me, book.

But the body, as usual, betrays. I have to pee. Urgently. Desperately. The more I try to deny it, the stronger the urge. Finally I interrupt Alex in the midst of his most tender lyric and leap out of the car, sprinting for cover. But where? Miles and miles of flat snow, not even a decent stout tree trunk in sight. I look back in humiliation towards the car.

Alex doesn't even have the decency to avert his eyes, but I'm beyond delicacy now. I hike up my skirt and bare my naked bum to the arctic winds.

When I get back to the car, Alex is waiting for me with a poem. He waves it triumphantly in my face like the victory flag he knows it to be. With one wave of Alex's magic word-wand I've been transformed from a weak-bladdered mortal to a goddess who rains her golden liquid into a parched and sterile world. The miracle of transubstantiation. "I've made you immortal," says Alex. He says it as a matter of indisputable fact. Simply, without bombast. I wouldn't dispute it anyhow. I know, at the instant of utterance, that it's true. My flailing, hollow self is again anchored to the only reality I can relate to — the reality of words. I feel alive, invested with meaning. Mythologized.

Alex's wife, Eve, was a beauty. An Ingrid Bergman beauty. I, on the other hand, was Jane Powell — but without the voice. And she was a sculptor. They lived with their bright beautiful daughter in a Hansel-and-Gretel house on the outskirts of Montreal which was the centre for a group of other writers and painters.

At my insistence, Alex asked me along to some of his Sunday-night gatherings. Compared to the craziness of the Sydney scene, this one was respectable, even stodgy. But that didn't bother me — I was much too grateful to have discovered a small pocket of familiarity in the midst of Montreal's frozen wasteland. What did bother me was that so many of those who gathered at Alex's house were Jews, like Alex. Jews with beards. Jews with paint on their jeans. Jews with ink stains on their fingers. Nothing from my past experience prepared me for the shock of this. In Australia, Jews were businessmen and their sons doctors and lawyers.

Occasionally, a more daring one ventured into the rather raffish field of architecture, but that was it. Period. Now I made the startling discovery that Jews were "low lives" too. What would Fanya have made of this phenomenon? But I didn't pause too long over the answer. Fanya was light years away and I was here, in Alex's sitting room; sitting in front of his fireplace; listening to poems being read, discussed, quarrelled over; sipping cheap wine. I felt that I had finally located the heart of the city. I was home.

Except that it wasn't home — not my home. This pretty tableau belonged to Alex and Eve. Again I was the Outsider with my nose pressed against the windowpane looking longingly at all the goodies inside. It was storybook time starring King Alex and Queen Eve and their brilliant court. I decided to crash through the glass. I too was entitled to a role — I would be the Wicked Witch. Screw the beautiful talented wife. Screw the pretty innocent child. My need was greater than theirs. I had discovered the Holy Grail without even knowing that I had been on a quest; I had finally found my Pinheaded Chinaman who would not only shake my hand but would be mine forever. Here, with Alex, was the synthesis I had secretly been seeking — the fever of words, books, ideas, and the security of home, hearth and Jew. And I sensed with the cunning and insight engendered by need that I could lay siege to the castle and storm it.

I looked at Eve looking at Alex and realized what she herself didn't realize — that she didn't believe in him. No, that wasn't quite right. Eve was too pure for him, too straight. A sculptor, she worked with real elements — stone, metal, clay. Alex inhabited what for her was the shadow realm of words. He sensed in her a contempt for its abstractions. In me, however, he smelt a fellow fanatic. There weren't too many of us around. Until I came along, he had a lonely task — to hold the world together with the sheer weight of his own beliefs. With me, he could afford to shift the burden just a little. There were two of us now —

two pairs of Atlas shoulders to keep the world from falling to pieces.

I launched my compulsion against Eve's complacence. Nietzsche was right. It was all a matter of will. My "I want" would prove more powerful than Eve's "I don't want." And I wanted Alex. His recognition would vindicate my life.

But where was Alex in all this? What was his role? His desires? His fears? Strangely enough, all of this was irrelevant. Alex — forceful, strong, dominating Alex — was the Virgin Prince, the spoil that would be awarded to the victor. Whoever exhibited the greater strength, the greater determination, would carry off the prize. She was Waspy and weak as a willow. I was Jewy and strong as a stallion. I started to bulldoze my way through their fifteen-year-marriage. Slowly, slowly, it began to crumple.

Every day after work we met at my apartment. Our bodies were so much alike — legs that looked as if they should be rooted into the earth, strong, stocky bodies, peasant faces — that making love to each other was like making love to oneself. But the fucking was only the foreplay. The *real* fucking was the talking. That's what we really came together for. We displayed our lives in front of each other like shrewd Jewish merchants in a richly stocked bazaar. We loved each other's wares; fondled and pinched and caressed the objects of each other's past lives. "I can't talk with Eve," said Alex. "She won't listen anymore. She closes herself against me." *I* couldn't open the lid of my life wide enough. Its jumble of rubbish spilt out around us. Under Alex's gaze, it turned into an avalanche of brightly coloured jewels.

I knew then that Alex was mine. Apart, we were mortal. Together, we possessed an androgynous power. The nightmares I had dreamed, the grotesqueries I had invented — I

124

offered them for Alex's use. I was a gold mine, a treasure trove for Alex to plunder. Since I didn't want these treasures myself, I was wild with joy that I had found, at last, someone who valued them.

I was also beginning to understand something else about Alex — that his greatest vulnerability lay in his refusal to admit his vulnerability to himself and to the world. I knew that Superman was really Clark Kent. I remembered it for him so that he could forget it. For this he was beginning to love me. For this he was beginning to hate me. For this he was bound to me forever.

—◆—

Scene: The den of the abortionist. Correction — the gynecologist's consulting room. He's Italian, a friend of a friend of Alex's. In the waiting room, not ten yards away from the table on which I'm lying spread-eagled, stirruped, ready to giddy-up and trot, sit at least eight heavily pregnant, lightly moustachioed Italian ladies, the floor between their swollen elastic-stockinged legs crawling with offspring. Fecundsville — and me the odd man out.

This is abortion number two, but this time there is no Fanya across the street to hide from, no Tom waiting for me. Although Alex has paid the shot, he can't be here with me "due to prior commitments." Yes, that's what he tells me — prior commitments, as if he's a very busy, very on-the-make politician. Which I guess he is when I come to think of it.

Am I angry at Alex's defection? Outraged? I must be, but I don't — I daren't — acknowledge it. Instead, I feel nothing. A sad sort of nothing. Alex can only fit me in the next morning for an hour or so. "We can go for a ramble," he says. A *ramble*? A pleasant little post-abortion ramble? Well, why not? Why the hell not? Just what the abortionist ordered.

I dive-bomb onto the suggestion, and instead of shrieking like a harridan, howling like a coyote, gibbering like an orangutan, I nod my head and smile a sweet bright sprightly smile. All of a sudden my life's ambition has shrunk to wanting to be able to walk briskly and cheerfully, so that Alex will admire my guts. "My God, you've got guts!" he'll say.

Next morning I'm there before he is. I stride along the path. Am I impressing him with my life force? Is he thinking of how gallantly I fly in the face of adversity? Yesterday lying under the knife, today dancing under the sun — or something like that. But I can see after two minutes that it's to be nothing like that. Nothing like that at all. Does he even remember I've had an abortion? "My poems," he declaims. "My genius . . . how could I be so great? I bow down before the altar of my beautiful exciting inimitable self . . . genius . . . Genius . . . GENIUS. . . . "

Eve was in hospital. She was having an abortion too. A legal one. It was her heart — she had a rheumatic heart. The timing was too cruel. It was the modern equivalent of a secret mistress having her bastard child in the gutter while the pampered wife gives birth to the legitimate heir in the family four-poster. Yes, that's exactly how it felt to me. I gave birth to my abortion alone and comfortless. Eve had hers amidst a flurry of flowers and Laura Secord chocolates. The X-rays showed gross cardiac enlargement. I didn't want to hear that. After all, I wasn't a monster. I'd have been satisfied with just a little bit of enlargement. Like not having quite enough breath to make love properly. Like being slightly crippled. Like losing just a touch of her beauty so that the battle could be a little more even. So that plucky Jane Powell could have a chance too. . . .

Scene: We're sitting in a restaurant, fumbling with our half-empty coffee cups. Alex's face is drawn. His waiting-in-the-wings position is becoming precarious. The battle has continued too long. But he still refuses to take any responsibility in the matter. The most he can do is to acknowledge that there *is* combat. Therefore, he has come to a decision — he'll let Eve make the decision. She has been collapsing under the strain, blaming him for the limbo which we have — all three of us — created for ourselves.

He is going to call her up this minute. He will put it to her straight. "It's up to you, Eve. If you want me, just say so and it will all be as it was." He fumbles for a dime, can't find one. I dig a couple out from my purse. They wiggle in my hand like silverfish.

Alex barrels over to the public telephone in the corner of the café. He looks like a boxer heading out into centre ring. His voice booms over to the booth where I'm sitting. "It's up to you, Eve. . . " he begins. My body is chilled, paralyzed. Only my eyes can move. They follow him as he comes back, more unsteady this time. He sits down. Silence. There's a strange blend of sadness, bafflement and triumph in his face. We stare at one another.

"She doesn't want me back," he says at last. "She hates me. I've asked her to take me back and she's told me no. It's all over between us. She's given me to you. I'm yours."

She's given me to you. . . . My whole life has hung in the balance of a woman's syllable — yes or no. Her answer could have been dictated by the fact that she was pre-menstrual, that she had run out of cigarettes, that she was having trouble with her work. . . .

Alex stretches out his hands to grasp mine. The unused dime falls from his palms to the table with a *ping*.

———◆———

I threw myself into a frenzy of apartment hunting. Not that this was discussed. Not that anything was discussed. Except it was understood that as soon as I had found something suitable we would embark on our new life together.

I scoured the city looking for a place that we — I — could afford, expenses being another matter we hadn't discussed. Finally I found a small first-floor apartment on a charming street off Côte des Neiges. It had an extra room for Alex's study (how I loved the ring of those words — "Alex's study") and a kitchen big enough to prepare all those delicious meals I had planned. It even had a minuscule verandah overlooking the back of the mountain which grew out of the city's body like a leafy hump. Even though it was minutes from downtown, the country atmosphere of the place made me begin to look on Montreal with a kinder eye.

The snow had almost disappeared and with it the winter of my discontent. I squirreled through the second-hand furniture stores on the Main. First, a desk. Bookcases. Then a brand-new double-bed mattress, but this time with the added luxury of a box spring underneath. The old mattress was sent off to the Crippled Civilians. From one Crippled Civilian to another, with love. Who was going to add new territories to its familiar map of stains? I wondered. Not that I cared. I needed a new mattress for a new life. Everything had to be as comfy and as homey as I could make it so that the shock of transition from the Eve-home to the Anna-home would be cushioned.

My new apartment was less than a mile from my old one but it was a lifetime away. I arrived at the front door ecstatic, and fearful, of starting life with Alex, who had also left his old home, had also packed his bags and said his farewells. Who was even now waiting to greet me at the start of our new life.

I slotted the key into the door. "Alex!" I yelled joyfully, ready to fling all my refugee packages into the air, ready to jump onto our brand-new mattress, the one we were going to bounce around on joyfully for the rest of our lives. "Alex!" Silence. It didn't take long to search out all the corners of our small apartment. There was no one here but me and that was no person at all.

In panic, in anger, I dived for the newly installed phone. "Hello, hello. Can I please speak with Alex?" "Sorry," answered Eve in a perfectly normal voice. No hint of the fact that her husband, the father of her child, had left or was about to leave the family nest to live with Anna, the Other Woman. "I'm sorry, I can't disturb him. He's writing." Listen, you bitch. You sanctimonious piece of shit, I wanted to yell. You call him to the phone or I'll smash your goddamn face in! Instead, I murmured, "I see. . . Well, would it be convenient to call him back?" "Is it important?" "Well, no — it's all right. It's okay. . . I guess I'll call him in a couple of days." "Who can I say is calling?" Carefully I replaced the receiver.

Tell him it's Snow White's stepmother. Tell him it's the Virgin Mary and I've just had a miscarriage. Tell him to boil himself in his own ink. . . .

The Adorable Amanuensis

Alex lived in two houses. Both were plagued. If there was a crumb of anguish and pain to be extracted from the situation, then Alex extracted it. He reminded me of those religious Jews who, at Passover, would go around the house with a candle, looking for the delinquent crumb of *chometz* which might still be lurking in a remote corner.

Alex looked in each hidden corner of his life for that delicious morsel of pain which had defied detection. Let it be found and held up to the closest examination. If it didn't exist in one household, then surely it existed in the other. Back and forth. Back and forth. Supper here, breakfast there. Each one of us trying to outvie the other in the grace and delicacy with which we regaled his meal times, his leisure times, his bed times.

Victory for me if I got to wash and iron the shirts. Victory for her if she gained possession of the intimacy of socks and underwear. Who was to receive the sacramental gift of Friday nights? Who, the intimate ordinariness of a Tuesday or a Thursday night?

But the prize, the most prized jewel in the Alex crown, was the typewriter. The hearth that sheltered that particular household god was blessed. How I feared and desired it! On privileged nights, I would secretly sneak up and stroke it as it squatted like a Buddha baring its mouth in a many-toothed enigmatic grin. Its absence left a void which seemed to suck into it all the premeditated coziness of the small apartment. The apartment was a bower, and I the thieving magpie who went out on foraging expeditions to bring home in triumph some small piece of coloured glass, a stalk, a twist of bright cotton. It was a prison nest — velvety with coziness, sticky with comfort — that I had created for him, the master word-spinner.

But I, too, was capable of spinning webs with just as much energy and dedication.

I couldn't keep away from Eve. I felt almost as bound to her as to Alex. The more contact I had with her, the more real I felt.

Telling her how sorry I was to hurt her was guaranteed to hurt her even more — spitefulness operates with enviable economy. I was still scared of Eve — of her talent and her beauty. I coped with my fear by turning it into hate; I coped with my hate by turning it into pity. Underneath we both knew — and this knowledge forged a peculiar bond between us — that I was out to destroy her.

Scene: I'm talking with Eve in her living room. "He's not a man at all," she says bitterly. "He's a sponge." "Maybe," I answer cleverly, "but when I press him, nectar comes out." "When *I* press him, I get dirty water," answers Eve.

She leaves the room to make coffee and I open a folder of her latest sketches which are on the coffee table. The top one is of a naked woman lying on her back on what looks like a butcher's slab. Her legs are wide open and up in the air.

In between them is a man, also naked, with an elephantine erection, his face buried between the woman's thighs. On both their faces there is a look of obscene devouring greed. The woman is unmistakably me, the man even more unmistakably Alex. The drawing is entitled "His Favourite Meal."

"Want a snack?" calls Eve from the kitchen.

—◆—

And so the game goes on. Pull, tug. Pull, tug. I'm stronger, so I'm gaining. I'm younger, so I'm winning. He's on my side of the line most of the time now. A few more heaves and he's mine.

—◆—

Scene: Alex is going to have supper with his wife and child. He's taking a shower which is always a suspicious sign. It means he's probably going to fuck Eve, although he may not be aware of it. In fact he probably isn't. But I am. And I'm stricken by panic. Not so much by the fact that he'll be screwing someone else but that I'll know the exact time and place of it. It is an unbearable knowledge. I can write the whole script — supper with the kid, a little family television perhaps. A heart-warming putting-to-bed of the daughter, and then Mother and Father get down to it. A look, a touch — and off with the clothes and on with the lust. A lust they haven't experienced for years, a lust given to them by courtesy of me.

I know all this takes place because each time Alex "goes home" for supper he comes back at dawn. "We were talking about the settlement," he says. "And I got so exhausted I fell asleep on the sofa and didn't wake up till now." Or more often than not — and worse — nothing. No explanations at all. My free spirit — what's left of it — doesn't demand such middle-class excuses but my insecurity does. It screams inside for reassurances, any reassurances, just so they are minimally believable. The trouble with Alex is not that he's a liar. I don't care about lies. It's just that he's such a bad liar and doesn't give me even half a chance to believe the lies I so much want to believe.

This time, though, I won't let him get away with it. I'll dry him up at the source. Render him incapable. Milk him dry. Literally. "I've never been a sexual athlete," Alex had said. "Once a night is as much as I can manage." Right! I fling myself upon him as he's getting out of the shower, ready to step into his briefs — the ones *I've* washed. And his shirt — the one *I've* ironed. I wrestle him down onto the dripping-wet bathroom floor. "Cut it out, Anna. I'm wet. I'm late." "Just five minutes. Give me just five minutes. I want you to fuck me. Now. I need it. I want it." Panic disguised as lust. "Wait till I get back then. I'll come back early and we'll make love all night long." Oh, yes! "No, no. It must be now. I want it now." "Anna, please. Come on. Anyway I can't, here on the floor like this."

Crafty as a water rat I realize that if I let him up and out of the bathroom he'll escape my compulsion which, as much as my weight, is pinning him to the floor. Fucking is out, that much I know. The circumstances aren't right. My head goes down to his crotch. Mouth rape. A reluctant soft worm stirs against my tongue. Softness. A vulnerable helpless softness. And then my mouth gets fuller and fuller. My jaws work mechanically. Unpleasant visions of an electric milking machine invade my head. Or of a snake farmer I once saw milking venom from the fangs of an adder. How is it possible that these images aren't being transmitted to Alex? But he's my creature now. Utterly in my control — that is, for the three and a half minutes it takes to make him come. Then and only then will I allow him to go free.

"Good-bye, my love," he says, tranquilized, pleased. "I'll be home early."

"Good-bye, darling," I say. "Enjoy yourself. It doesn't matter when you're back. I'll be here."

Fool! Fool! The innocence of the male which is his most potent weapon. The knowingness of the female which is her saddest failure. . . .

Scene: No, he can't get divorced from his wife. It costs too much, and anyway who wants it? I do, whines a high-pitched insistent voice which I recognize with surprise to be my own. He'll buy me a wedding ring, though. It will be a day filled with fun. First we'll pick up Nathan, our "best man," have lunch at an expensive French restaurant and then go to a jeweller. . . .

I'm a vision of loveliness in a white seersucker dress scooped low in front and edged with white curtain bobbles at the hem. Nathan is in a rusty-black pin-striped three-piece. Alex wears a creased rust-coloured shirt and a grubby pair of bottle-green corduroys held up by a plastic belt.

A discomfiting thought surfaces. I'm heaving all my compulsions at Alex, but they could just as well be aimed at somebody else — it's the compulsion not the partner that's vital. The partners are, in fact, interchangeable. If the compulsion fits, wear it. And my compulsions fit Alex with an almost frightening perfection.

But I squash such dangerous thoughts. I'm in love. We go into a little jewellery shop on Mountain Street. I make straight for the ring section. I've earned my right to this outward token of recognition through months of frustration and confusion, and I mean to have it.

There are three trays of gold bands on the counter. I try them on and hold my finger up to the light, just like the lady in the jewellery shop ads. But wait a moment — there's some vital component missing from the picture. Where is the hovering, adoring, slightly sheepish male? Where is My Fiancé? Surely he can fulfil my fantasy projection on this, my day of days.

But the groom is on the other side of the shop. His face, bending over the showcase, is grave and intent. "I'll have that one," he says to the deferring proprietor. A heavy silver bracelet is removed from its velvet nest, the price tag discreetly brushed aside as if it were an irritating accessory. Money changes hands, the package is slipped into a side pocket. "Okay, let's go," booms the groom.

I falter. I stare. My tongue cleaves to the roof of my mouth. My right hand forgets whatever cunning it knew. "But, Alex. . ."

"Just thought I'd pick up a little something for my wife. . ." his voice rumbles and he lets fly an electric bolt of a smile at the proprietor who flinches visibly under its charge. "For the wife, you know. This'll look good on her. She'll love it. Have to keep the ladies happy, ya know."

Yes, Alex. Yes, of course. But if that's the case, then what's this fast-rising pool of blood I'm standing in?

Nathan — who is known as a honey-tongued traducer of female flesh, a man who even as he says "I lie" is lying and who can no more give up his sweet lies than a bee can give up its nectar — even Nathan looks stricken. He grabs a gold band from the tray, pays for it with a wad of notes and pushes it onto my fourth left-hand finger.

With this ring I thee wed. With this ring I thee bled. . . .

Alex is going noisily insane over in the corner. His voice bellows into the fragile air. The sonic boom is enough to raze all Montreal. No. All of Canada. It will blight every single maple leaf from sea to shining sea.

As I stare at my be-ringed hand, it detaches itself from my wrist and minces daintily on its five fingers towards the exit. Nathan bows and with a flourish opens the door.

Just before the hand reaches Mountain Street, Alex lassos it with the bracelet. It collapses inside its silver prison and dies. The only thing left alive is the band of gold which flashes out a Morse code to the indifferent passers-by — "V for Victory. V for Victory. V for Victory. . . . "

The Pain Machine finally ground to a halt. Eve withdrew from the game of three-man rounders. She went to Vancouver with her daughter, leaving the field to the two dedicated players.

I was ecstatic with relief. I had managed to pull off a neat trick, although doubts assailed me as to how I was going to maintain it. I laid them aside. I'd won! Now the typewriter, like its owner, belonged to me. And the manuscripts. And the reams of typing paper and the sharp pencils and the erasers and the dictionaries and the books. They all lived where I lived. So did the writer. I was complete.

Alex is mine. Montreal is mine. I am mine. Nobody has blamed me for the breakup of Alex's marriage. Nobody has snubbed or ignored me. On the contrary. I'm the charming, bright, clever girl in the starched Snow White dirndl all over again. A small, chubby, brown-skinned, blue-eyed, fair-haired sweetheart.

And in September I am to start teaching literature to high school girls in a Westmount private academy. No longer will I be peddling books — now I will be paid for teaching them. The best little literature teacher; the best little literature wife.

I'm the literati's love, Montreal's darling, its pet. The

fair innocent maiden thrown into the den of the literary lion to placate its fury. The sacrifice.

What nobody knew was that being Alex's victim was a way of ensuring that he was mine.

"How can you bear living with him?" asks a lady professor at a cocktail party. I simper, raise my eyes towards heaven and look as much like a pre-Raphaelite version of the violated maiden as I possibly can, given my Jewish peasant looks and my Australian sturdiness.

Yes, the literati loved me. They could afford to. I offered no threats. I was the Adorable Amanuensis.

I couldn't believe how well my life was going . . . until the night Alex came home at 3:30 A.M. smelling of expensive French perfume. Reeking of it. Great billowing clouds of it curling in and out of his armpits, crotch, from between his fingers, behind his ears. Had he visited a perfume factory? I inquired politely. Or fallen into a vat?

"I bumped into an old acquaintance in a coffee shop," he answered, sincerity oozing out of his voice like warm mud. "And she ran up to me and hugged me. I guess her perfume must have rubbed off against my jacket."

I had had exactly six weeks to enjoy my ill-gotten gains. Off with the Barely Old, on with the New. From Child Bride, Keeper of the Sacred Typewriter, to Discarded Wife. Anna into Eve. Queen Bee to beetle in one small step. . . .

I came to Alex a naked kewpie doll like those celluloid ones my mother used to buy for me at the Royal Easter Show. He dressed me up in a staggering variety of costumes — Daughter, Mother, Ball Crusher, anti-Christ, Lilith, Little One, Maidel-Paidel, Sweet Ass, Handmaiden to the Arts, Endearing Companion, Avenging Fury.

How comforting it was to have my roles, like so many freshly laundered dresses, laid out for me. Who was the servant? Who the served? We never stopped playing long enough to find out. I mimed each role to perfection. I was flawless in my devotion to the craft. From each according to his ability, to each according to his needs — we were the perfect Marxist equation. Endless abilities, voracious needs. Alex called the changes; I leapt into the spotlight, dressed myself up in the costume he had laid out for me, bowed to my audience of one and commenced my performance. I was Trilby to his Svengali, Joan to his Darby, Beatrice to his Dante. . . .

There were times, of course, when the perfection of the equation broke down — I wanted to remain Endearing Companion, for instance, whilst Alex needed me to play Avenging Fury; I remained hopelessly stuck in my role of Ball Crusher, ignoring all the signals for my change to Sweet Ass. But such anomalies were few and far between. Alex wanted; I wanted him to want. I needed him to want. I had no reality except in his imagination. Words for Alex were the magic spell by which he rescued himself — and me — from the terror of the outside world. He told me the fairy stories I wanted to hear. Hearing them I felt inviolate; my boundaries were delineated. I had substance, character, definition.

He thought, therefore I was. . . .

Wherever Alex was, whatever he was, had to be perfect. Imperfections terrified him. This gave rise to a confusing syllogism in my mind:

Alex's world is perfect
I am part of Alex's world
Therefore I am perfect.

But I knew only too well how horrifyingly imperfect I was. Something was wrong with my reasoning and I couldn't figure out where the error lay. . . .

When Alex wrote a poem, I sat with him, his most obedient help-mate, and checked the thesaurus, the dictionary, the encyclopedia. He asked me to choose words, to suggest titles, to compare versions. If he stayed up all night, so did I. I was totally engulfed in his process. He was writing me. He was me writing. If I left the room, the poem ceased to exist. I was all the children in the world clapping the magic into existence.

When, finally, the poem emerged whole from the type-writer, I had to memorize it. If I failed to get it word perfect after three or four times, either there was something wrong with the poem or there was something wrong with me. I was never quite sure which was which. When I could recite it flawlessly, I was rewarded by a pat on the head or a fuck.

"I am a poet," boomed Alex. "I eat up the world and I'm greedy. Everything I do is for my writing. If you like my writing, you must like everything I do. I'm right even when I'm wrong."

"Yes," I agreed. "I am your handmaiden. I am your Muse. You can do anything you want. Anything."

What I meant, but was too devious to admit even to myself, was that he could do anything *I* wanted him to do.

A Piece of the Alex Pie

Hella — Our Lady of the Perpetual Perfume. It was every-where. I was drowning in the rich pungent fumes of French perfume. An expensive way to die. Could anyone have devised a more perverse torture? My heart started to beat violently as soon as Alex put his key in the lock. I couldn't rush up to him anymore, couldn't hug him spontaneously. Instead I approached him haltingly, sideways, like a paraplegic crab. If I moved slowly, maybe it would give the perfume time to go away. Or maybe I'd be lucky this time and it wouldn't even be there.

I approached, sniffed, like a bloodhound on the trail. Sometimes the perfume reached out and hit me like the heavy blow of a mallet. Sometimes it teased me with its faint elusive whiff. Now I smelt it, now I didn't. If I wasn't sure, I'd wait until Alex had taken off his jacket. Then when he wasn't looking I'd sniff at his discarded clothing with a sick intensity. If that didn't yield the desired/undesired effect, I'd sneak out of bed at night and sniff his underwear like a pervert. I could never work out my desires — did I want to find the perfume there or didn't I? If I found it, my loathsome behaviour would be justified; if I didn't, I'd feel relieved. Either way I won. Yet I was overcome with shame at my hateful activities, full of self-loathing and anger. My life had become a hell. I was dancing on the end of another woman's perfume stopper. Somehow in all of this, Alex had become reduced to Mittelmensch. He was merely an instrument for my torture, a carrier of the plague.

With the perfume came the poems. To the Perfume Lady. To Hella.

"I'm a poet," said Alex. "I need Experience. I need to Embrace the World. And anyhow, what's the problem? It's all in the head, all in the imagination. Nothing's real."

Nothing except my pain and confusion. Since Alex wrote me into existence, he could, by writing about another, wipe me out with one lethal stab of the pen. . . .

At least if I had a worthy rival. Or so I told myself. A raven-haired silky-skinned doe-eyed beauty. Then my own unworthiness would have been confirmed — my vulgarity of spirit, my triteness of mind, my dumpiness of body. That I could understand; *that* I could measure myself against and find myself wanting. Or so I told myself. The rejection would have been clearly defined in breast size, brain size, luminosity of skin, elevation of ass, superior moral values, etc. etc. There would have been pain but it would have been short and quick and clean. Not like the murky swamp of being supplanted by a Hella. If she were Numero Uno in the idiosyncratic mathematics of Alex the Creator, then where in god's name was I? Off the end of the yardstick. In limbo. That's where. . . .

Hella. "Her life is a Greek tragedy. Ask her up for coffee." So pronounced St. Alex of the Apocalypse.

The Greek Tragedy arrived in an apricot angora sweater, tight black leather skirt and plastic sandals with see-through stiletto heels filled with water in which swam a single plastic goldfish. Her ankles flashed gold chains, her conversation clattered with clichés. If her life were a Greek tragedy, then surely Hella was the Goddess of Vulgarity.

But there was one attraction which Hella possessed against

141

which I was powerless — she was an Authentic Survivor, a Jewish war orphan. She had lived out my adolescent fantasies. Her life, like Alex's, was printed in capitals.

Hella's parents were killed in the Warsaw ghetto. She escaped because she looked like a typically pretty Polish girl — broad Slavic features, blonde hair, tilted nose. She spent the war years dodging around from house to house as a kitchen maid. Once she was assigned to clean a German officer's apartment. The address was a familiar one — it was her former house which was being used as a high-ranking officer's billet. The officer turned out to be handsome and he played Bach divinely on the old family piano. Hella fell for him. She lived out the rest of the war humping her German soldier in the high brass bed in which she had been conceived — the touch of depravity which was needed to put the edge on what would otherwise have been just another Holocaust story.

Within two years of landing in Montreal as a war refugee, she had met and married a plump rich manufacturer, a maker of fashion mannequins. She even started writing a book about her wartime experiences. Alex would bring me chapter after chapter and ask me to comment on it. What could I say? What could I feel? I had sat at home in Australia having my concentration camp fantasies and browning my well-fed limbs in the sunshine, while Hella had Survived. She could easily have been one of those skinny frightened children to whom I had passed out bowls of scalding soup as they got off the boat in Sydney.

I didn't feel lucky or privileged to have escaped. On the contrary, I felt the victim of a geographical accident. My childhood experiences had been filled with terror too, but my sufferings somehow didn't count, were not authenticated in the eyes of the world.

Now I sat with Hella's manuscripts, reading of her war experiences and wishing they could have been mine. Except that I would have written them better. The ordinariness of Hella's imagination couldn't begin to rise to the events which had been visited upon her. Her prose was guaranteed to set one's teeth on edge.

Unless you were Alex, in which case it was guaranteed to give you a hard-on.

You were born circumcised, as you never tired of telling me. When the *mohel* was called in, he made only a ritual cut because God, that Great *Mohel* in the Sky, had already done the job on his favourite child. Because of this, your mother treated you as someone special, one of God's favoured children. Like Moses, she would say, you were born to lead your people; and rather than circumvent God's sign, she treated you with caution and respect.

"A very special prick," you'd say, waving it around in front of me. "A prick which has received special treatment in heaven and therefore requires special treatment here on earth."

There were times — too many times — when I wished that God had sliced the whole damn thing off while he was at it. Life would have been so much simpler for both of us. . . .

Enter the Ecstasy Twins — at least, that's what I called them. He was the largest and noisiest of Alex's acolytes, and she his lady. It seemed that we could do nothing, go nowhere, without them. They were with us at all times. "Ecstasy!" yelled Robert as he barrelled through the door. "The artist

143

is the prophet of ecstasy. The artist is the lightning rod shoved up the asshole of the bourgeoisie. The artist is the risen Christ, Moses leading his unenlightened followers into a land flowing with tropes and metaphors. Art! Life! The Cosmos!"

Against that energy I was numb. Dumb. The three of them — Alex, Robert, Nina — lunged themselves against the wintry wastes of Montreal, hair, scarves, words flying from them at all angles. Flying into the frozen, ox-like faces of the passing Philistines, who by some horrible mistake dared to walk the same streets, inhabit the same city. I stayed at home, clearing away the coffee cups, feeling like a fizzled-out piece of slag which had accidentally come into contact with fiery coals but which stubbornly refused to become ignited.

"What's wrong with you?" shouted Alex, when he returned from his walk, glowing like a neon light. "We're too much for you, eh? Too much energy for you to cope with. What do you think of them — my spiritual children? Bursting with talent and joy and poetry — and I've created them. They're my best poems!"

Yes, Dr. Frankenstein. Yes.

Years later I heard that Robert had had a nervous breakdown and was incarcerated in one of the more discreet sanatoriums in Montreal; while Nina, after confiding in me that Robert had been impotent throughout their entire affair, converted to Catholicism.

The infuriating, the unforgivable thing about Alex was that he was never there. Never. Even when he was. My existence was totally at the mercy of a telephone call, a knock on the door, a letter. He was everything from a one-man industry to a multi-national corporation. Demands from everywhere, from everyone — they all had to be satisfied, none could be denied. The more distant the relationship, the more urgent the need for intimacy.

I was nailed like a bat to a barn door by anyone's random desire. Enormous gifts of time and energy were bestowed on those who meant little or nothing to him. On Joyce, who wrote letters (he always answered them the same day); on Caroline, who wrote bad poems (he compulsively tinkered around with them); on Sheila, who was having massive problems with her MA thesis (he wrote the whole damn thing for her); on Moira, whose three children were taken away from her under mysterious circumstances (he tried to make her pregnant by compensation); on Sally, who was threatened by a hysterectomy. There was even a woman who placed collect calls from Halifax at 3:00 A.M. — Alex couldn't refuse her either. He accepted the charges as if he had no choice in the matter and then listened while she hurled violent obscenities into his ear.

He was willing prey to a whole army of female predators although he fulminated endlessly and passionately about the demands these women made on his time. There was anger, real clotted anger, in his voice. "They can't let me alone. They won't let me write, these stupid selfish bitches. They all want a piece of me. They're tearing me to shreds. They don't care for my poetry. They don't care for me. All they care about is grabbing something for themselves."

Yes, but where was I in all this furious flurry? Where or what was the centre? It all seemed to be a mad whirling useless periphery. There had been a cruel, ironic reversal of my status — when I was on the periphery of Alex's life, I was the centre of it; now that I was at the centre, I'd been thrust back to the periphery. I seemed to get only the left-overs — if there were any. The harpies pressed in on him, shoved me aside, elbowed me out, until I began to have fantasies of

hacking my way through the crowd with a bright sharp
machete.

—◇—

"Can't you see?" explains Alex in one of his gentle fond
moods. "They all get a piece of me but a piece is as good
as nothing. You get my core, my real self."
   I do?? Then where is it? Help me just once to locate its
position and I'll hold fast for a lifetime and not budge.
Meanwhile, until that happens, screw the core. I'll gladly
make do with a piece of the Alex pie. Any piece. I'm modest
in my demands.

—◇—

"I'm here!" bellows Alex as he bursts through the door after
a week's absence. "I'm here! Who called me? Who wrote to
me? Where are my messages? Where's my mail? I'm *here!*"
   Like fuck you are. . . .

—◇—

Alex flew high and when he landed he needed a landing pad.
I was his landing pad, but the trouble was he didn't always
trust me to be there. What if the wind blew me to one side?
What if, in a fit of perfidy, I moved away and he was forced
to take a pratfall? What if there was a crash landing? There
were a thousand and one emergencies, a thousand and one
contingencies; therefore the need for a thousand and one
landing pads.
   The landing pads had names. They were called Hella and
Susan and Betty and Jenny and Leila and Sandra and

Roberta and Lucy. Alex set about organizing them with the manic energy of an obsessive collector. They had to be there to cover every conceivable occurrence he could imagine — and then some. I knew that when everything was plain sailing, I was the preferred landing pad but that wasn't the point. No one told Alex — and he couldn't seem to find out by himself — that one landing pad encouraged precision on-target landing; many encouraged a dangerous carelessness.

Alex was terrified of the power of women. That's why he surrounded himself with them — they defused one another. There was safety in numbers — or so he thought.

Scene: We've been to a weekend conference in Kingston, Alex and I. Some friends from Alex's university — Harry and Ruth — have offered to drive us there and back. Although Alex rarely asks me to go on literary jaunts with him, he can hardly object to this one. I love meeting Alex's literary friends. It makes me feel good, gives me a feeling of solidity, affirms my place in the sun. Everything goes well until we get ready to drive back to Montreal. Christine, one of Alex's "mature" students — she has been attending the conference as well — asks if she can get a lift with us. "Sure thing," says Alex, beaming from ear to ear. "No problem."

Our friends innocently nod agreement. No problem, except that the car is a tiny one and the three of us will be squished together for the four-hour drive back. Christine, Alex and me.

An hour into the drive, with dark falling rapidly and the humming heat of the car making us all a little groggy, I sense something which makes me jolt upright with tension. Alex and Christine are all over each other, hands up skirt, in crotch, down blouse. There are gasps and sighs and moans. I must be imagining this. And so I sit quietly in my allotted third of the back seat, directing all my energy to blotting out what I know is happening less than six inches away. I can open the door and fling myself out onto the highway; I can stab Alex in the groin with my sharp pen; I can shriek my head off. But I dismiss all such thoughts from my mind. Instead I become a hostile silent collaborator.

Harry and Ruth, who aren't aware of the back-seat drama, turn around to say good-bye when we reach our apartment building. "A great drive in, eh? Nice and smooth?"

"Great!" booms Alex. "Simply great!"

As soon as we get through the front door, Alex makes a lunge for me and kisses me passionately. I am shaking with anger, but at his touch it all dissolves into lust. I pull him to the floor, tear off his clothes and ride him furiously.

The Shoe of the Shrink

If my body had been as slow to respond to pain as my mind, I would have watched my limbs drop off with gangrene, my teeth blacken and rot, ulcers proliferate. I would have been an admiring spectator of my own disintegration, commenting with fascination on my own decay. "What brilliant colours! What subtle sensations! What unusual texture!"

After a time, I did respond to the peculiar notion that I was hurting, and with that finely honed negative-sense bloodhound nose of mine so brilliantly trained to sniff out the worst possible solutions, I sought and obtained the services of a psychiatrist. He was, without any doubt, the sickest shrink in the business. Or, as Fanya would have put it, he was not a well man. The minute I entered his office I knew I had the upper hand and that I would maintain it. I sensed weakness in the air like a particularly nauseating brand of after-shave lotion. Expensive after-shave lotion.

Leo Farber was about four-foot-eleven with watery-blue myopic eyes; bald pate with a scraggly ring of greying hair which hung to well below his thin sloping shoulders; sunken belly. On this pitiful frame hung Mexican shirts — the sort only North American males wear — and jeans which managed to be at the same time too tight across the hips and too baggy in the ass. He had tiny offensively trim feet, shod, with a truly nasty nattiness, in an astonishingly versatile assortment of pastel suede shoes. Thus my psychiatrist.

He was smart, that I'll grant him, but I was smarter. Which for a patient is stupid. After all, I was not giving him my money or my time in order to dazzle him with a show of wit and insight. Nor was I sitting in his office in order to prove to myself in fifty minutes or less that I could fool him. Or was I? What really kept me going was the fact that I had conceived a gigantic lust for this weak, unattractive, uncharismatic creature. It wasn't really lust, as Dr. Farber explained to me as I sat drooling in his black leather chair. It was projection. Leo Farber's modest function was, it appears, to represent All Men. And in the psychiatric lexicon, All Men translated into One Man — Father.

Had I come full circle? My life, far from being a progress, however slow, from point to point, was only a frantic sideways jump from one circle to another. Here I was lusting after Feivel again! What a bugger to have been born Jewish! Had I been lucky enough to be a Catholic, I would have been able to fuck God the Father happily ever after and even been applauded for my piety and devotion.

Projection or no projection, Dr. Farber was no help at all. He was, in fact, madder than I had at first thought. To begin with, he had a fixation about shoes — not mine, his. At the beginning of every session, he'd whip out a pair of brand-new shoes from a box which he kept under the couch and thrust them into my face for approval. I wouldn't have minded so much except that after a while I began to resent the fact that these shoes were being bought by my hard-earned money — I was supporting his habit. Question: Did he take me on as a patient to earn extra money for his shoes, or was his shoe obsession engendered by my particular brand of neurosis? We began to spend more and more of my expensive time discussing what these shoes meant to him in terms of our relationship. I offered him, free of charge, many clever and varied interpretations — he was trying to boot me out; he was trying to establish his dominance; he was trying to seduce me, his feet being his downwardly displaced genitals.

The latter was, as it turned out, the correct explanation. Late one night there was a knock on my apartment door and a drunk and reeling Leo Farber stumbled into the living room. Not only was he drunk, he was high as a kite on amphetamines — his pockets were stuffed with them. Pulling out fistfuls of pills, he flung them around the living room, laughing like a maniac when they skittered out of sight under the furniture.

Taking a look around to make sure I was alone — I was, as usual — he raced over to the window, yanked it open, pulled off his boots, hurled them into the snowy street below and took a flying leap across the room to where I was sitting. Pinning me to the floor, he tried to rip off my clothes. Luckily, since I weighed more than he did, I was able to free myself.

He popped a couple more pills, stared at me in silence for about five minutes, then unloaded the thoughts he was obviously unable to tell me in our sessions.

"Alex Jacobs is a cunt!" he yelled. "A selfish cruel egotistical prick!" (A part of my mind noted and disapproved of Dr. Farber mixing his metaphors.) "But we all know this, don't we! Everyone in this fucked-up universe knows this. What they don't know, Would-be-wife-of-fucking-genius, what they don't know is that you're just as big a prick! Just as big a cunt! You're an angry bitch. A queen-sized angry son-of-a-bitch! You're angry at me, at that poor prick-faced Jacobs, at your parents, at everybody in this goddamn world. But most of all, at yourself. So you attach yourself to that pathetic pain-in-the-goddamn-ass poet so that no one will discover your dirty little secret. So that you can be so goddamn superior to everyone. Well, I've found you out. I've goddamn found you out!"

He took a deep breath and stared at me again. I stared back. I was amazed, outraged, furious. I was also admiring. My dumb doctor had finally broken out into something which even I had to recognize as being perilously close to the truth. I waited to see if there was going to be any more. But he was finished with me and into a different scene.

For the next two hours he gave a wildly inspired performance of a man undergoing electric shock therapy. Marcel Marceau could have done no finer. Jerking spasmodically, he threw himself on the floor, foaming at the mouth, gnashing his teeth, pulling at imaginary electrodes, all the while keeping up a high-pitched gibberish that was horrible to hear. It was a brilliant and frightening performance, one which I was scared to interrupt since it had the trance-like quality of sleep-walking.

Finally, when it became obvious that he had worn himself out, I covered him with a blanket and let him sleep it off.

Just as dawn was breaking, he woke up and started in on me again. His face was haggard, his tone gentler and sadder. "When are you going to face yourself, Anna? When are you going to face your own anger? That's what it's all about — *your anger* — and as long as you're with that poor son-of-a-bitch Jacobs, you'll never get rid of it. He's perfect for you, isn't he? The perfect shit. You can rely on him to do all the wrong things. You need him to justify your anger, don't you? But it's all too neat, Anna. Too neat and too dangerous."

I was far too tired to listen. Besides, I didn't want to hear. I sent him home with a pair of Alex's spare boots. And as soon as his office opened, I called his nurse to cancel further treatment.

Scene: I'm sitting at the kitchen table waiting to participate in a religious rite. Alex is about to hand over a poem he has been working on. For the past few hours he has been muttering to himself, drumming his fingers to beat out the rhythms. The muttering has become louder and louder, the drumming more frenzied, until the final shout of "It's a masterpiece!"

Alex triumphantly brings in the finished product as if he were a High Priest offering a giant communion wafer to a humble penitent. It's a love poem to Hella. I know that immediately because that's what it's called — "Love Poem to Hella."

"What do you think it means?" asks the High Priest, a Jesuitical gleam in his eyes. "Figure this one out if you can."

For me, keen little student that I am, the task is simple. I have been well tutored. The man, I begin, symbolizes the Artist; the woman, the World. The theme of the poem is the need of the artist to submit himself to the experience of the world. That is its larger context.

Father Jacobs nods to me to continue. I'm doing well. I now proceed to break down the poem into its components and analyze it line by line. Even I can tell that I'm outdoing myself. I'm flushed with success.

Alex is obviously pleased. Then, a look of displeasure crosses his face — there has been a small flaw in my exegesis, a minor misinterpretation. Taking the poem from my hand, Alex proceeds to lecture me, patiently but with condescension.

Quite unexpectedly — I surprise myself by the suddenness of it — I explode. "The poem's about fucking! That's what it's about. It's about a cock — *your* cock — going into a cunt — *her* cunt. That's what it is and nothing else!"

And before Alex's outraged eyes, I start ripping up the page. I throw the shreds into the air and they come falling down on us. Confetti to bless the holy union of Alex and Anna.

I couldn't wait for Alex to get out of the apartment so I could prowl around like a Scotland Yard detective. I sifted through the contents of his desk; bloodhounded my way through his papers, clothes, even the books in case there was a tell-tale poem written on the flyleaf. Inevitably there was. The evidence of those poems was my undoing. I now knew for sure that dressing-up time was over; that I was stuck in the one terrible role of Harridan Wife and imprisoned there, seemingly for life. I was undone by a stanza.

The worst, though, was when I listened in to Alex's conversations on the extension phone. I didn't mind when Hella called him "darling." That I could bear. The pain came with hearing her call him "bastard" and berating him viciously for forgetting to send flowers for her birthday, for being careless about appointments, for not paying more attention to her in public. Anybody could claim the intimacy of endearment; only intense involvement gave one the right to insults. . . .

Pain Junkie

After eighteen months, it was time to move, time to set up house again. If we had a "proper" place, we'd be a "proper" family. NDG — that was my target. Notre Dame de Grace. No Damn Good. Yes, but that was a silly Montreal joke. NDG was the perfect district — as solid and staid as any burgher or his wife could wish.

I found a third-floor apartment with large sunny rooms, which looked just like a house. It had an old-fashioned wooden-railed verandah, a fireplace that worked, and there was no one on top of us or to either side. I entertained visions of baking apple pies in the kitchen, roasting chestnuts by the hearth in the winter, swinging lazily in the hammock on the verandah in the summer.

The very first night we moved in, Our Lady of the Perpetual Perfume arrived. She presented one red rose to Alex which she extracted from the steamy warmth of her bosom to "warm the house."

Oh, the perfidy of the female sex! Oh, the perfidy of the male sex for accepting and swallowing the perfidy of the female sex!

One thing about the new apartment which I had forgotten to mention was that it was less than five minutes away from where Hella lived. Coincidence? Choice? Who could tell? Was I sick or was I healthy? Was I innocent or was I guilty? Where did neurosis leave off and good healthy accidental circum-

155

stance begin? Perhaps it was better to assume, like most shrinks, that it was all neurosis and proceed from there.

What remained, however, was the solid incontrovertible fact that Hella was dancing the tango with Alex in our newly acquired living room. The rose was clenched between her teeth in some absurd parody of an Apache dance. She leaned back over Alex's arm and fluttered her eyes. In passion? In nervous anticipation of falling flat on her back?

And what was I doing, little household drudge, little Ella by the Cinders? What did Cinderella do when her Prince Charming danced with the Ugly Sister, who for some inexplicable reason was actually quite attractive?

What she did was put the record back on when it was finished so that they could go through another erotic round together. . . And disappear into the kitchen to pour some coffee for refreshments and apologize for the lack of cake. And then she went into the bedroom and surveyed herself in the full-size mirror which, in a moment of domesticity, Cinderella and the Prince had just that afternoon fixed to the closet door. She looked into it and the glass swirled with mist just like a bad horror movie. Reflected in it she saw a dumpy frumpy teenager with bandy legs, thick waist, featureless face. In the background was another image — Feivel sitting in a sagging armchair rigid as a totem pole while from around the back of the chair protruded the smirking face of Fanya. She threw me a hideous mocking wink but her eyelid remained gummed over one eye. She couldn't lift it open. In an effort to loosen it, she jabbed her chin viciously into Feivel's shoulder just like Alice's Duchess, and for no reason commenced to giggle — an awful obscene phlegmy giggle.

I whipped my eyes away from the mirror image to look behind me at the reality of the room. But I was too late. My parents, cleverly anticipating my move, had zipped into the living room. I knew they had, because I could hear my mother's giggles coming from there. The record had come to a close and was going around and around and around in the groove. No one bothered to change it. . . .

Scene: I'm skimming through some books in a store on St. Catherine Street to see what I can get for my students. I come across a name on the spine of one of them. It catches my eye — Julius Axelrod. He's an Australian. I buy the book and later that night I start reading it. Yudel, it's you!

I read with fascination all through the night — I can't put it down. It's like seeing myself through a looking glass, spying on part of my own childhood.

You have it all down, Yudel — your hysterical mother, your brutal disappointed father, your forbidding Zayde. How they made your life a hell, how they damaged and marked you for life. Everyone is there except me, Yudel. I was the ghost at your miserable feast. Everyone was out to get you, out to destroy you. What you didn't acknowledge or — unforgivably — didn't remember, was that *you* were out to get *me*. It was you, you neurotic little shit, you, who made my life a hell and marked me for life. But, no — not a mention about your peeing on me, about your chasing me down every back street of St. Kilda, about your spitting out Yiddish curses or putting the boot to my dolls.

On the back of the book jacket is a photo of a sensitive, interesting-looking man sucking on a pipe; on the flap is a quote from a prominent critic who calls you a brilliant writer.

Yes, Yudel, you are a good writer, but it really pisses me off that you make literary capital out of what were *my* childhood memories too. Hey! I feel like yelling. I was there too!

There's no one more possessive of bad experiences than a writer.

Tom McCarthy, my first lover, is dead. He was found on the piss-stained floor of a public telephone booth, the receiver still clutched to his ear. Had he been trying to make one last obscene call to Fanya? The note from Archie Atkins said he had OD'd on methedrine. Although he had been out of my mind for a long time, the news made me shudder.

I began having the common nightmare of an expatriate Australian — finding myself back there without a return ticket and no likelihood of being able to earn it. "God!" I would mutter through clenched teeth. "Why did I come back? Why did I put myself at risk? How did this horrible thing happen?"

I would wake up from this dream drenched in sweat and look through the window at the falling snow to reassure myself that this was Canada, this was Montreal. That New York was less than an hour away by plane and Europe seven hours away. That I was safely not at home.

But instinctively I moved away from the radiating warmth of the person I was sharing a bed with. I didn't want to be a part of it. Until I realized that the spilling black hair on the pillow next to mine belonged not to my mother but my lover.

When summer came, Alex decided to go to Paris. He needed to experience it on his own.

Alex's plans to spend the summer alone wounded me deeply. But the old habit of rationalization reasserted itself — Alex was not going on something as banal as a holiday. It was a pilgrimage. An odyssey. Others might gather rosebuds; Alex gathered Experience.

I saw him off at the airport, smiling bravely through my tears. Even when I got back to the empty apartment, I refused to give in to my pain.

Gil, who lived in the apartment downstairs, came over to console me. And together we plotted to escape to Never-Never Land. Whenever we were together, we were able to erase our unhappy childhoods and start all over again. He was Peter Pan and I was the young Wendy. We were going south of the border to make a pilgrimage to all the towns and places that had been part of our adolescent mythology — Santa Fe, Laredo, the Badlands, the Petrified Forest. Once we had left prosaic unmythologized Canada behind us, we were also going to make love. If God was going to take a leave of absence, so then was the Keeper of the Eternal Flame. I prepared to deliver myself, body and soul, into the hands of the Philistine.

On the night before Gil and I were due to take off, our bags already standing in the hallway, a telegram arrived. "COME," it said. There was no denying its imperial summons. Down the drain with Gil and all our brave plans. Wendy was a grown-up now. . . .

When Alex met me in Paris, he handed me a three-page poem about my arrival. Written, of course, before he had even sent the telegram. Upstaged again! Welcome back to Literary Landscapes, Anna. Welcome back to the Land of the Undead.

Summer is over and the song of self-pity is heard in the land. Whine, whine, whine. Days of whine and poses. Is anyone chaining me to myself? To Alex? I can get up on my own hind legs, as Fanya would say, and walk away, can't I? But of course I'm just playing around with the notion. I'm Fanya's daughter, a pain junkie, cruising around for a fix.

I'm fused to Alex because he has the magic and as long as I can manage to hold on, I can possess it too. I can't manufacture it on my own. I can only borrow it — that is, steal it —

from him. Alex knows this and I'm determined to make him pay for that knowledge. I threaten, I rant and rave, but I stay.

Stone walls do not a prison make. Until you put them into a poem, that is.

Scene: I'm standing in front of the class of "my girls." My special hand-picked ones. The sensitive vibrating literary girls who are glanced at askew by other members of the staff as likely trouble-makers but who are my particular pets. My darlings. All of them are reincarnations of me when I went to school. We read Blake and Dostoevsky and Lawrence and we go — in schooltime — to see jumpy print revivals of Eisenstein and Jean Renoir.

I'm Miss Brodie. But with a difference — my prime is gloriously ahead of me. I *live* with Literature. Which means that I live with *Life*. Sexual frustration isn't going to point me in the direction of fascism and "my gels" know it.

This day I'm passing out xeroxed copies of De Sade's *One Hundred and Twenty Days of Sodom*. All faces are turned to me, all attention riveted on my words. I'm everything a literature teacher should be — enthusiastic, passionate, compelling, involving. All of a sudden the stream of words stops. Dries up. I stare at the class. I know nothing. Absolutely nothing. I have nothing more to say. I'm overcome with the sudden revelation that I'm a fraud; that I know nothing about anything which is worth knowing about; that every single girl in front of me knows how to live life with more grace, more dignity, more self-respect than I've ever possessed or am ever likely to possess. There they all are, staring up at me, waiting for me to start dazzling them again. But dazzle time's over. I throw De Sade down on my desk with a bang. "Get out your grammar books," I snap nastily at their puzzled faces. . . .

160

Scene: "Red Rose!" bellows Alex. "I want more Red Rose!" We're in bed, making love. At least that's what I think we're doing. But it isn't me Alex seems to want but rather the cloying sickly odour of Yardley's Red Rose cologne. Somebody who thought she was a friend gave it to me as a casual gift. I hated it right away. It was the sort of smell a refined English lady would have chosen to leave behind her in the toilet, had she been given the choice.

Alex is besotted by its genteel sickliness. Is this the wifely alternative to Hella's heavy French seductress scent? Am I condemned forever to play Red Rose to her Joy?

Not that I spend too much time asking myself these questions. Not that I spend too much time asking myself any questions. I jump out of the warm bed, run into the bathroom, run back freezing into bed again so that Alex can make love to a bottle of cologne. . . .

If it's not Red Rose it's the phone. Can't we ever get to make love without interruptions? Br-in-ing! Leave it go just this once, Alex, I beg silently. Get on with it — finish what you've started. What could be more important than making love to me? What could be happening at the other end of the line that's more fun than what's happening in bed? Everything, it seems. "It might be God wanting to let me know he's made me archangel," says Alex. "Or King Gustav calling to tell me I've won the Nobel Prize."

Alex says it so convincingly I almost believe him — I *do* believe him. But it never is. It's always some lady wanting him to read her latest poetic effort or to help with a paper on CanLit or to meet for "a cup of coffee."

But still I go on believing whatever you say. Part of it is my need to believe, but most of it is your own unassailable belief in your own fictions. That's why I can't live without you. I can never quite believe in my own fictions — somehow they never ring true enough. But yours come across to me as the true gospel. Even to me, Woman of Little Faith, as you call me.

The trouble is, Alex, I have too much faith. That's why I resent you, that's why I hate you even as I love you. When you take away your fictions and give them to someone else, it wipes me off the slate.

———◇———

Scene: Nathan, my "best man," has persuaded me to take a little dab of acid. He has brought it up from Zihuatanejo where it has just been made. The cult hasn't happened yet. I'm absolutely terrified, but my terror at the unknown is outweighed by my terror of the known. It can't get worse and it might get better.

I dare to risk Alex's presence. He won't take it because, he says, he already knows what it's all about — his whole head is an acid trip; he's above and beyond any experience which an invisible dot on a handkerchief could possibly bring him. But he's all for my taking it. Maybe it will open my head to the extraordinary experiences with which he lives on a daily basis. Maybe it will unlock the tightly shut door of my understanding.

I take it. Or rather, I pass my tongue over the corner of the cloth that Nathan indicates is impregnated by the magic ingredient.

Alex sits in the leather chair watching me. I watch him watching me. And then he's no longer watching me. He's turned into a totem pole. An immobile impassive totem pole covered with snakes and great winged birds. Not frightening. Not threatening. Just *there*. Which is just as well because I don't want any interference. I'm too busy examining the living room of my apartment. I am appalled. The room is filled with containers. I'm not hallucinating. I'm just seeing for the first time what is really there. Dozens and dozens of round cylindrical objects with nothing in them beyond the occasional clump of dried flowers. There are shells and gourds and pots and baskets and vases and hollowed-out stones and nets and bottles and mugs. There's even a hollow skull. I have painstakingly collected these objects which have come from all parts of the world. From Greece and Portugal and Spain and Guatemala and Israel and Morocco. From Australia and Thailand and Indonesia.

What am I supposed to be doing with all these things? Am I to spend the rest of my allotted life span trying to find objects with which to fill these hollow containers? Is this supposed to be the purpose of my life, its focus?

Control. Contain. That's what my apartment says. But control *what*? The totem pole sits impassively in the leather armchair. Surely I'm not meant to fill all the hollow spaces with that.

A recurring nightmare: The books which fill up our apartment to overflowing are alive. Their thick, porous pages need to inhale oxygen to keep them from drying up, disintegrating. They suck greedily at the air in the room. There are thousands and thousands of them — a whole army — and only one of me. I can't compete — my one pair of lungs is totally insufficient. There they sit, the books, waiting silently on the shelves. Breathing. Slowly. Deeply. In with the oxygen, out with the carbon dioxide. I fight for the last suck of nourishing air. I'm panic-stricken, desperate. . . .

I wake up, gasping for breath.

"Where are you going at this hour?" asks Alex, as I fling on my dressing gown.

"For a breath of fresh air," I reply and dive for the front door. I make it out into the open just in time. . . .

One Greedy Gulp

My father died of a heart attack. While reading a book on the living-room sofa, he just fell back and died. Fanya collapsed and couldn't attend the funeral, and my family decided to spare me the trauma. I received the news from Aunty Sonya after the funeral.

I felt removed from Feivel's death. Since I had ceased to acknowledge his existence, I felt no need to acknowledge his non-existence.

But I was faced with the dreaded task of notifying my Montreal relatives.

"Nu, so how come you're keeping yourself a stranger?" Bronya asked when she heard my voice on the phone. "I have to hear about you from others?" Her tone was heavy with meaning. She had obviously heard of my affair with Alex, which was no longer a secret.

I escaped by telling her the news of my father's death. Bronya was heartbroken and insisted on calling the family together that evening. Everyone came, including the five little brothers of whom Feivel had been the eldest. They all looked so much like my father — the same mild expressions, the same inward-looking eyes with their almost willed indifference to the world. For the first time since hearing of my father's death, I felt bereaved, deprived of the father I had never known.

Until late into the evening we all sat around Bronya's kitchen table. "Oi," she said, "what a tragedy. A *tsadik* he was, your father, a real saint." And she and the brothers told tales of the brave and handsome man they had not seen for thirty-five years, a man full of adventure and life and daring. It was like listening to a fairy tale.

Just as I was getting up to leave, I found myself telling them the story of Aunty Milly's death. When I came to the part where she lay in her hospital bed, shrunken like a mummy, I felt an insane bubble of laughter deep inside my gut. It grew larger and larger until finally it burst out of my mouth in ugly brays. I couldn't control myself. I shrieked and rocked. I wet my pants. Tears rolled down my cheeks. My relatives were aghast. The table rocked with spurts and explosions of laughter.

Through my tears I had a nightmare vision. In the middle of the table was a saucer. In the saucer was my tiny yellow naked Aunty Milly, her lump of a liver pulsing. My laughter rocked the saucer, made it dance on the table. . .

That night I dreamt I had taken the saucer from the middle of the table with my Aunty Milly in it, sprinkled her with sugar and swallowed her whole in one delicious greedy gulp. After I had finished, I tried to wipe away some sticky crystals of sugar which stuck to the sides of my mouth. They wouldn't budge.

A month later I received a phone call from Fanya. Her voice came humming over the long-distance wire, high and hysterical. I was catapulted back to my childhood. Guilt skittered around inside my skull like a cage of trapped rats. . . . My God, I've forgotten to do the borders. . . . I've invited too many friends over. . . . I haven't turned the kettle off and the bottom's burnt through. . .

"Annale, tell me the truth. I'm your mother. I care for you. I'm going mad with worry. You're killing me. I want to know the *truth*."

Yes, Mother. All I can think of confessing is that the cupboards are a mess, I haven't rinsed out my bra in weeks, no one in her right mind would eat off my floors. . . .

"Annale, I've heard from the family that you're carrying on with a married man. You can tell me the truth. That's what a mother's for. *Anything* you can tell me. A married man! Oh my God, what's happening in your life? A mess your life has become. Tell me. Tell me. I've had a bad time since poor Feivel . . . but still you have to tell me."

A wave of relief washed over me. Was that all she called me about? My panic subsided, my fear drained away. The sins of my adulthood were nothing. They didn't count. The true ones, the ones that really mattered, were those that had been committed in childhood. . . .

Drawing on the "little nest egg" she had inherited from Feivel's life insurance, Fanya bought a plane ticket to Montreal to see for herself what was going on. Her most frantic fears were confirmed. Her daughter was living with a Married Man — one, moreover, who wasn't making appointments with divorce lawyers every day of the week and wasn't engaged in acrimonious financial struggles with a bitter discarded spouse. He was also that dread creature, a writer, and therefore immediately classifiable as one of her daughter's "low lives." But wait, there was something different here, a sweet new element — Alex was a Jew. Married, true, but a Jew. Her finely honed instinct sensed his genetically inbuilt weakness. Before her role as Jewish Mother, history would force Alex to revert to being a Jewish Boy.

"I want you to promise, Alex, that you'll take good care of my daughter. That you'll be good to her. Look after her."

Significant looks were hurled like poisoned arrows in Alex's direction. I caught myself almost feeling sorry for him. In ten minutes Fanya extracted what her insecure, screwed-up daughter couldn't have done in ten years — a promise of a quick divorce, a quicker marriage.

"Yes, Fanya," said the Wild Poet. "I promise, Fanya. I love your daughter and I'll look after her."

I felt tempted to enlist my mother's help in extracting a promise from Alex to give up *shtupping* his various mistresses, but I suspected that was going a little too far.

Fanya and Alex nodded their heads sagely in unison; fond looks were bestowed in my direction. I was discussed in the third person. Hey, wait a minute — what's going on here? It was Mummy-and-Daddy time and I was the little girl.

I'll fix you, I thought. I took Fanya to celebrate Krishna's birthday at the local Hare Krishna temple. I wanted her to feel as uncomfortable as possible, and at first I thought I had succeeded brilliantly. The incense fumes, the garish decorations, the scrawny little plucked-gosling figures trying to dance themselves into a state of ecstasy with their bluish shaved heads, frayed running shoes, tatty saris, tinny hand cymbals — confronted with this, Fanya nearly turned tail and ran.

Instead, seeing that I was determined not to notice her discomfort, she resigned herself to the inevitable, and went up to a couple of Krishna men. Quite courageous, I thought, under the circumstances. After a few minutes of animated conversation, she called me over. She was beaming. "Anna," she said, "I want you to meet Harvey Moskowitz. And this is Stewie Schwartz. Both from Brooklyn." Triumphant, she turned and hissed in my ear in case I hadn't gotten the point, "Jewish boys!"

From that moment on, Fanya was in her element. As far as she was concerned, it could have been Krishna's Bar Mitzvah. I could hardly persuade her to leave. She chattered away to the lot of them and it turned out that they were practically all Jews from New York State. How marvellous! How logical! What more perfect way for a good Jewish boy to take revenge on his good Jewish mother than to become a Hare Krishna devotee and exchange *yarmulke* and *tallis* for shaven head and sari.

Ah, if only there had been a Krishna boy around when I was growing up, I would have leapt upon him (making sure, of course, that he was not the Jewish variety), banged away on my tambourines, tinkled my little bells and sashayed my way through the city streets offering incense to all my mother's respectable friends. . . .

Once my role as daughter was firmly re-established, my mother bloomed. She became energetic, alive, even radiant. An ironic reversal — mother supplanting daughter. She flirted outrageously with Alex, insisted that he dance with her. And for the first time, she assumed the role of fond, permissive, doting mother. I hated every moment of it.

After she had returned to Sydney, mollified by events in Montreal, Alex told me that she had confided in him that I had been an impossible child, was not to be trusted with money and had suffered all my life from chronic halitosis.

Alex and I got married. It was quick and easy. No objections from Eve. We went to Ottawa to avoid a religious ceremony in Quebec. And this time Nathan was our true best man.

Fanya sent a telegram, and my family in Sydney got together and bought two dozen trees to be planted in our name in Israel.

I'll be smothering you. Alll-wa-ys,
With a love that's cruel. Alll-wa-ys.

Scene: We're visiting Alex's mother, Rivkah, who lives in the Jewish Home for the Aged. It's on Esplanade Street, not far from where my Aunty Bronya lives. Alex's mother, who is in her late eighties, thinks I'm Eve, but she wouldn't care even if she knew I wasn't. She's only interested in Alex. *"Gib mir dein hant,"* she whispers to him. Without waiting for a response, she snatches his hand and thrusts it down the front of her chemise. When Alex tries gently to withdraw it, she refuses to let it go. Instead she clamps it there against her breast and shoots me a malevolent look, full of fierce triumph. The expression in her eyes reminds me of my great-grandmother.

A woman called Martha started writing passionate demanding letters to Alex. She lived in a little industrial town in Ontario with six daughters and a cruel insensitive clod for a husband. When she was eight months pregnant with her first child he gave her a vicious drunken kick in the belly. The child — a boy — was born dead. She had become pregnant every year since, trying to get her son back, but it didn't happen. Nothing happened. She was burnt out. Her life was ashes. The only spark was Alex's poems. The only hope of a flame was Alex. Her unanswered letters ground on and on, unceasing in their demands. Why didn't he answer? Why didn't he care? Why didn't he rescue her, Prince Charming, and kiss her into her rightful state of princesshood?

I grew to hate her. Alex was there for *me* to make demands on. She was poaching on my territory, and, god knows, there was little enough of it.

After the first twenty letters, Alex weakened, as I knew he would, and took the fatal plunge. The letters flew between them like those of Abelard and Heloise, with me hovering in the background secretly hoping that Alex would meet Abelard's fate.

One night, sick of my passive role, I decided to jump into the act. I wrote a passionate demanding letter to Martha's husband. It was a parody of Martha's original letter to Alex, but I didn't expect him to know that. By return mail I received a parody of Alex's first letter to Martha. The man, far from being a clod, was witty! He was intelligent! He was literate! With any luck he'd be charming and handsome as well. Before long, Eddy and I were out-lettering Alex and Martha by two to one. And then one day I looked out of the window and saw coming up the path a warm vital attractive dark-haired woman and beside her a washed-out grey little man. He looked like a stick insect. I knew without a moment's doubt that I was looking at Martha and Eddy. Given the lopsided equation of my life, it figured only too neatly. She was coming to claim *her* lover, and he was coming to claim *his*.

In the end, it all turned out as I had known it would. Martha joined the firmament of satellites that revolved around the Alex sun. Eddy simply disappeared. . . . Finis. End of story.

Screwballs. Sickies. Idiots.

I don't even know who to be jealous of anymore. I've lost track. And anyway, I can see clearly enough through my confusions to know that it's the jealousy that counts — the causes are incidental.

I look after my jealousy, guard it, fan it if it looks as if it's in any danger of subsiding. . . .

I say love but I mean hate. I say jealousy but I mean self-hatred. I say fidelity but I mean possession.

Scene: "Peter has asked me to go to New York with him for the weekend," I say to Alex, presenting him with an imaginary fait accompli. Alex doesn't look up from the exercise book he's scribbling in. "That's nice," he murmurs. And then, almost as an afterthought, "Who's Peter?" "Somebody I met when you were away. I'm going to go with him."

It's clear to me that Alex is not exactly wild with happiness at this information. It's equally clear that he's not crushed either. He hasn't forbidden me to go, nor has he pleaded with me to stay, so I feel obliged to follow through on my non-existent plans with my non-existent lover. Luckily, a journalist friend of mine from Sydney, Rosie, is in New

York on a one-year working permit. She's been asking me to visit for months. I phone her to tell her I'm coming. I lay elaborate plans for my departure, packing an overnight bag in Alex's presence, simulating a phone conversation into a dead phone, projecting an air of nervous excitement.

But I *am* nervous. Nervous that Alex will discover my guilty secret.

Scene: Saturday morning. Somebody has just phoned with an important message for Alex. He's been in Toronto for a reading and if I call his hotel quickly I may be able to catch him before he leaves for home. "Hello, may I talk to Alex Jacobs, please?" "Sorry, ma'am, but Mr. and Mrs. Jacobs have just checked out." I put down the receiver gently, walk into the kitchen, take down the sewing basket from the top of the fridge and remove the scissors. Then I walk into our bedroom, open Alex's closet and systematically proceed to slash and cut into ribbons every garment he possesses. I hesitate for only a fraction of a second when I come to a very expensive black velvet jacket I had chosen for him only one week before. I overcome my hesitation, though, and slash a jagged vent through the left lapel.

I'm sweating and trembling with a terrible rage. And swearing. The English language, which I have hitherto admired and revered, now seems poverty-stricken. There just aren't enough expletives to relieve my feelings. In desperation, I start spitting out made-up words of my own — "Fluck! Crunt! Fross! Twack! Shrok!" Where is it all coming from, this rage? The intensity of it frightens me. I feel in danger of my skin bursting open with the pressure of it, my eyeballs popping out and rolling around on the carpet like glass marbles, my pores gushing tiny geysers of blood.

My hands move quickly through the hangers. Slash! Tear! Rip! Through the white heat of my fury I note that Alex

172

has more clothes than I have. And more expensive ones. This adds to my anger but I tuck the information into a corner of my mind to be examined at a later time.

My slashings have refined themselves. I'm no longer cutting indiscriminate holes in everything. I'm confining my activities to making neat vertical slashes in the flies of Alex's pants and, with surgical precision, excising the zips. They lie on the floor all about me like limp skeletons of tiny snakes.

Exhausted, I collapse onto the floor amid the debris. Three hours later Alex returns and finds me there. I haven't moved. He stares in horror at the ruins of his clothes. I raise my head, look at him through swollen red eyes. "Which one is Mrs. Jacobs? Which lucky lady won the jackpot this time?"

In a flash, Alex understands. I can almost hear him making quick-as-lightning calculations. Should he become enraged? Protest his innocence? Pretend ignorance? To my surprise, he does none of these things. Instead, he bends over me and helps me to my feet. "Clever girl," he says fondly, "it's about time I had a whole new wardrobe anyway. How about washing your face, making yourself pretty and then we'll go shopping for some new pants and jackets. Some really *good* ones this time, eh?"

I'm totally disarmed. I have no defences against this strategy. "Okay," I reply in a voice so meek I surprise myself, and we walk out of the bedroom arm in arm.

Strange Reasons Why I'll Never Leave Alex

Strange reason one: We're travelling by train through the Peloponnesus, Alex and I. I'm jumping out of my skin with excitement at the spectacular scenery flashing past the windows. Alex remains seated at the far end of the carriage, scribbling into a notebook. Stubborn. Stolid. I can't bear

173

what he's doing; I can't bear what he's missing. "Look," I yell at him in frustration. "You're missing everything. You're missing the world. Come and *look*!"

Alex raises his head slowly and stares at me as if I'm a piece of bargain-basement furniture which has irritatingly and inexplicably become animate. "*You* look," he says coldly. "And after you've finished looking, I'll read you a poem and let you know what you've been looking at."

"I'm leaving him," I say to myself behind clenched teeth. "That's it. It's all over. Finished. I'm living with a death's head."

Half an hour later, Alex reads me his poem. Within seconds, everything I've seen, everything I've felt, vanishes. Alex has taken the landscape, the reality, and made it his. And by reading his poem to me he has given me the supreme gift of his vision. I'm swamped with gratitude.

"Now do you understand?" he murmurs tenderly, looking at my mesmerized face. "You look, but I see."

Strange reason two: I've just heard from Sydney that a girl friend has died. The news stuns me. I run to Alex, telegram in hand. I want him to comfort me. To hold me. To stop my sudden and awful loneliness. He hands me back the telegram. "Too bad," he says nonchalantly and walks out of the room.

"I'm leaving him," I say to myself behind clenched teeth. "That's it. It's all over. Finished. I'm living with a death's head."

Sometime later, Alex brings me a poem he's written about my friend's death. My grief begins to melt. The thought strikes me that somehow her sudden and untimely death is redeemed by the words on the page.

—◆—

"Can I help it if I bump into a heavily perfumed woman in the street? Am I responsible for the entire female world of perfume users?"

No matter that his affair with Hella was now in the open, no matter that he wrote poem after poem about her and dedicated them to her at public readings, Alex still refused to admit it. It was a magnificent sleight-of-mind since it enabled him to achieve two important things simultaneously — he convinced himself of his own innocence and he turned me into the hypocritical nagging shrew he needed in order to justify his defections.

"Fuck her as much as you like," I screamed. "Fuck her silly. Just tell her not to wear perfume when she sees you. Or if that's too much to ask, leave a change of clothing at her place."

"Fuck who? What perfume? You're suffering from olfactory delusions."

"Here. Smell for yourself, pig." I rammed a wad of dirty laundry up against his nose. "Smell. Inhale."

"Smell *what*?"

It didn't seem to occur to either of us to enlist the aid of a third nose, to call on an objective outsider. We were both too hopelessly locked into our follies. And, anyhow, Alex needed me to do exactly what I did just as much as I needed to do it. Neither of us wanted to be sprung from our pre-cast concrete roles. That, after all, was what my function in life was — to be a function of someone else's.

What a relief it would have been if only Alex had remained faithful to his Artist as Ubermensch stance. But unfortunately he was betrayed by a most unsuperman-like guilt. It undermined my role — I could only play martyr to a genuine god, otherwise it was all a cruel farce. Alex, alas, couldn't stay fixed in the role he had chosen. He betrayed himself through weakness and guilt.

Genuine male evil, genuine wickedness, commands some sort of perverse respect from a woman — it disarms. Male

175

weakness, never. It undercuts, undermines, fills the woman with contempt. A dependent contempt. . . .

Scene: We're at a small gathering at Hella's place. It's for the publication of Alex's latest book. I don't want to be there but I feel I'd be churlish if I refused. At the back of my mind is the thought that if Alex sees how relaxed and carefree I can be, he'll realize how superior I am.

Halfway through the evening Alex stands up and delivers a speech. He names everybody in the room and describes in moving terms the special place each holds in his heart. Then he pulls Hella to his side, puts his arms around her and expounds on her unique and admirable qualities. My name is not mentioned. The guests are squirming with discomfort, shooting me quick glances of sympathy. Hella is beaming, purring like an overfed tabby.

Absurd dialogue: The grand finale. The bed — our bed — is reeking with perfume. "Alex," I shriek, "it's on the bed now. The goddamn bed is full of Hella's perfume." For the first time I want a denial, I need a denial, but Alex, predictably, does the perverse thing and turns the tables on me. "Yes, I know." I'm dumbfounded. "You *know*?. . ." "Yes, Hella was here."

I'm all geared up for a battle I thought I was familiar with. Now I'm on foreign soil and will have to regroup my energies. "What," I say, "were you doing on our bed with Hella?" I am talking very slowly. Soon I am going to hear the answer I want and dread, soon he is going to tell me that they were making love, that they were fucking. Reality. Finally. After all this time. I welcomed it. I dreaded it.

Everything winds down into slow motion. I watch closely as Alex opens his mouth. Here it comes. The moment of truth. "We were reading David Daiches." Now Alex's mouth has stopped moving. It's time to open mine. Even I am astounded at the idiocy of this answer. I'm disappointed, hurt even, that he hasn't bothered to think up a more plausible story. "David Daiches? . . . " I question tentatively. "Yes, you know, poor Hella. She's working so hard on her literature paper. She called up crying. Said she needed to look up something in Daiches' *History of Lit*. Which, as you know" — a pedantic conspiratorial nod towards me — "is a first-rate piece of work. So she popped over and we spread the books out on the bed — two damned heavy volumes — and I helped her look up all her references."

A pause, during which I feel my mouth become a corkscrew. Our dialogue is rapidly turning into something out of the Theatre of the Absurd, into bad Pinter. I play my part flawlessly. "Why didn't she take Daiches out of the reference library down the road if she needed it so badly?" The reply comes razor-sharp, fast as a flash — Alex is quick on his feet this round; I have to admire his athletic reactions. "She tried to. They were out." "No, they aren't, as a matter of fact," I reply deftly. "Oh?" "Yes. Just as a matter of the purest coincidence, I checked them out this morning on my way to school and they were there, sitting on the shelf."

I challenge Alex to turn my truths into the lies they so palpably are. If he does (and he knows the rules of the game as well as I do — he should, he invented them), then I'll be allowed to do the same with him. No. The play must go on. "Well, by the time Hella got there this afternoon they must have been stolen. You know what it's like with library books. . . . So they've gotten around to stealing old David Daiches' books, eh?" A knowing chuckle is interspersed here, for comic relief. "When will they get around to stealing my books from the library? That's the ultimate compliment. . . . Hey! I've just had a wonderful idea. How about you stealing my books from libraries and bookstores and then they'll have to keep reordering them. How about it, eh? Let's get cracking on it. How about starting right now, eh?"

How about cracking your jaw open with one of your own hardbacks?. . .

"Listen, you shit. David Daiches was not stolen. Those books are there. I know because I checked them out on my way *back* from school and they were there in the library." "Then the librarian must have had them off the shelf to rebind them." Alex is in great shape today, top of his form. "They're new, shmuck. The Daiches books have just come out. Why would they need to be rebound?" Triumphant rejoinder by Alex; he knows he's about to win the round. "Then that's why Hella couldn't find them. They were cataloguing them because they'd just come in. God, those librarians take their time. What sterile bitches they all are anyway. Frigid custodians of passion."

I know when I'm beaten but I still have the energy left for a last riposte. "I'd hardly call David Daiches a purveyor of passion. . . " "Oh, I don't know," muses Alex, warming to the subject. "Sometimes critics can reach such heights of insight that they can become creative themselves. Creative criticism, that's what it's called. The Critic as Creator . . . not bad . . . not bad. . . "

Now I *know* he's fucked Hella on our bed. If Alex can be forced to such conclusions, then I can only guess at the depth of his guilt. To my amazement, though, I begin laughing like a maniac. What the hell is David Daiches doing in our lives? Our conversation has been totally insane. *We're* totally insane. Screwballs. Sickies. Idiots.

I fall back onto the desecrated bed shrieking with uncontrollable laughter. Alex falls on top of me and we both roll about in the perfumed sheets, gasping for air, hugging each other, doubling up in huge spasms of laughter at the craziness of our dialogue, at the craziness of our lives together. . . .

When we made love, I came for the first time in months and Alex didn't once mention Red Rose. . . .

The Poem Machine

The David Daiches episode released me into a promiscuity I had almost forgotten I possessed. I discovered a whole new world outside the claustrophobia of my life with Alex. Once beyond that rapidly shrinking space, I felt myself expand with a newly acquired power. I found that I was in possession of a whole new panoply of tricks, compelling new tricks with which to display my sexual credentials. I now became the one men sought out to get a literary buzz. Without being aware of it, Jane Powell had metamorphosed into Georges Sand. I went out into the world armed with intimate literary perceptions.

Literature was sexy. I used it the way some women used perfumed douches. . . .

Michael. My lover. He was thin, gentle, worried-looking and vulnerable. If there existed such an entity as an Alex-Opposite, then clearly Michael was it. However, since my psychic economy insisted on having an Alex in the equation, I devised an ingenious solution — I became Alex. And since Alex couldn't function without his partner in the balancing act, then Michael must become Anna. I engineered the transformations with ease. I made a splendid Alex. I expostulated and strutted and made Michael analyze the real Alex's freshly minted poems. If he failed to get a good mark, he failed to get a good screw.

Michael, unfortunately, made a pretty lousy Anna. One evening when I presented him with a poem, he exploded. "Get that bully boy's puffed-up crap the hell out of here!" I flung him a look of outraged scorn and sent him packing.

After that experience, I decided to keep the affairs cool and controlled. To my surprise, I discovered there was no lack of takers.

Alex was angry at my having horned in on what was, indisputably, his act.

"What you don't understand," he said, "is that I'm not promiscuous. I need to feed on life the way a vampire feeds on blood. For my work. Experience! I need to suck it dry, but then I always toss the rind away and come back to you. . . . But you — you're the Philistine, the anti-Christ, Lilith, the Destroyer of Men, Kali."

"Don't have anything to do with me," I warned my lovers in a low sexy voice. "I'm Lilith. I'm Kali. I'm the anti-Christ." But they only clamoured for more.

The ploy that was to be my salvation began to pall. I was bored; the game lacked tension, excitement. I didn't want any sensitive discussion afterwards, any soul searchings. I didn't want any psychic temperature taking. I just wanted the man to wield his sexual machinery efficiently and leave the field.

But after a while the division of labour sickened me. All that raw material and no Art! All that flesh and no Spirit! All that meat and no potatoes! Where was the miracle of transubstantiation? I was at home only with Alex. He was the only one who didn't bore me. The only one who was cleverer at the game than I was. Whose lies were his truths. Whose falsities were his fidelities. Whose rationalizations were his reasons. It was an irresistible brew.

Alex — the Compleat Solipsist. He filled his world with intricate multi-faceted constructions. They revolved around his blazing centre and threw back to him brilliantly coloured refracted images which never ceased to delight and amaze him. These images were equal and interchangeable since it was Alex — and only Alex — who gave them meaning and light. Their functions remained fixed — only people were expendable. Some people, it was true, fitted better than others, performed at a higher rate of efficiency — these had a lower rate of attrition. There were some — very few — who were given tenure. Others, especially those who became too ambitious and tried to extend their field of action, were ruthlessly searched out and destroyed. Plucked out of God's blazing firmament, they were cast into the oblivion of outer darkness.

Alex was a One-Man System. "No one can make me happy," he pronounced. "And no one can make me unhappy. Only I can do that for myself. Others can be responsible for my comfort or lack of it, yes. But only that. Nothing more."

I envied him. His infallibility was more inviolate than the Pope's. He, Alex, was undisputed God of his universe, an ever-expanding one, God's energy being infinitely renewable. The world was Alex's dream. When at brief intervals he awoke, both he and his Creation fell into a state of chaos.

It was then that I confirmed my function, my place in the Great Scheme of Things. It was just as I had known from the start — Alex would never leave me. When he awoke from his solipsistic dream to nightmare reality, he needed to be able to reach out and touch me. I was his reality. What irony since I could not be my own reality. I think I envied him that too. In the Dreamworld other people were pawns for Alex to move around at will. In the Realworld there was only me.

I was unique. I was irreplaceable. Without me the universe was in danger of cracking wide open.

My function confirmed, my place assured, I no longer had need of lovers. But neurosis abhors a vacuum and something Other immediately rushed in to fill the emptiness — I became obsessed with living space. Suddenly our apartment began to feel stiflingly inadequate for our needs. I had to have a house. A proper house. One that a family lives in; one that could be featured in *House and Garden*.

My obsession was fed with the news that Alex had been awarded a literary grant. He wanted to use it to buy time and write. *I* wanted to use it to buy a house and live — or try to.

I didn't care about the cost. I didn't care about the fact that our apartment was cheap and comfortable and accessible and pleasant and perfectly suited to our outward needs. My inner needs said "No." My inner needs said "Change."

I found myself believing — truly believing — that if I discovered the perfect house I'd be the perfect person. What did I mean by the perfect person? What did I mean by the perfect house? I had no idea but I was sure I'd recognize it when I saw it. All I knew was that it had something to do with an overgrown tangled garden, fireplaces scattered at random throughout the house, the odd sloping roof, at least one exposed brick wall, an oak beam perhaps, an attic study. An extra bedroom, or two or three, for the unconceived babies. Add to this one Alex, one Anna, and suddenly happiness, laughter, harmony would start sprouting from every pore of our skin, every corner of the house. A pipe would grow from Alex's lips, leather patches from his elbows; an apron would flower at my waist, delicious aromatic brews bubble from the stove.

Through the magic circle drawn around our front porch only benign fairies would pass. The evil ones bearing poisoned fruit as their house-warming presents would not be able to penetrate. Everything would be solid. No cracks in the corners, no chinks in the chintz. Maybe Alex could even practise a little accountancy or dentistry on the side. . . .

Alex could have his pile of words; I wanted my pile of bricks. We struck an infernal bargain — one among many such bargains.

My life became a ferment of house agents, house hunting, house bargaining. I had firmly made up my mind to be upwardly mobile — to graduate from the stodgy respectability of NDG to the seedy gentility of Lower Westmount, Upper Westmount being far beyond even my compulsions.

Again my unique ability to sniff out disaster came to my aid. After months of looking, comparing, weighing and evaluating, I found the worst house in Montreal. It was a parodic inversion of my fantasy, a diabolical mirror image, like those wishes made on a monkey foot. Yes, it had an attic — but with sloping floors instead of sloping ceilings. Hansel and Gretel windows? Yes, but as airy-fairy and insubstantial as the spun-sugar confections of the witch's cottage. A romantically tangled garden? Yes, but with a romantically tangled tree whose roots sent cracks right up through the foundations of the house.

On this rock I am founding our lives. On this rock I am foundering our lives. . . .

We were two sick and charming children, Alex and I. I bought the house because deep down I knew it would be a disaster; Alex bought the house because the owner had, on his bookshelf, a couple of his books.

The minute we were in, I wanted out. I didn't even have the grace to wait until the ink had dried on the mortgage contract. I wandered the hilly streets of Westmount late at night, peering in through lighted windows. There in *that* house, in *that* room, under *that* roof, swinging in the hammock on *that* verandah, toasting our toes in front of *that* hearth — that's where our perfect happiness lurked. Only it belonged to others. Always to others. Never to me. My perfection was constantly eluding me. I prowled the streets like a marauder, crouching beneath windows, peering into shrubberies, pressing into doorways. I ran back to Alex with frantic breathless reports. Houses. Houses. HOUSES!

I invented a brand-new compulsion — domomania. I'd finally discovered it — the perfect torture instrument, meting out pain and anxiety in even-handed measure to both of us. An ideal neurosis, one that I could control, unlike Alex's which only *he* could control. This one was all mine. I had invented it, taken out the patent. I hugged it, nurtured it, clasped it to my bosom, foul asp that it was. Its poison wasn't fatal. On the contrary, it was self-regenerative.

We got rid of our first house at a considerable loss but no matter. We were now into our second. Obsession Mansion. But Alex couldn't deny me my obsessions because I allowed him his. The old infernal trade-off. Tit for tat. Literally. In this house there were rooms to burn. Six no-nonsense bedrooms, all of them large and draughty and serious about demanding occupancy. In the wacky logic of my head it all figured perfectly. The extra bedrooms would engender the babies to fill them up. Since space existed to be filled, then the getting of the space would ensure the filling of it.

Primitive magic. First the fantasy, then the fact to fit the fantasy and then the fact to fit the fact. To me it all seemed simple; to our friends it appeared slightly demented. "You need a large house like a hole in the head," they told me. Precisely. I *did* need a hole in my head and if one didn't exist I tried my best to create it. . . .

———<>———

Everything I did fed into a poem, everything I said. I was a poem machine and Alex the Master Technician. All my neuroses — even my house-mania — were grist to Alex's poetry mill. I guarded them fiercely — they were the main-spring of my power, the source of my significance in the Alex-Cosmos.

Along with this realization came a growing sense of resentment. Alex made use of my fears, my craziness. He was an incubus feeding off the blood of my nightmare-self. I felt diminished, plundered. But there was also a little voice in the back of my mind telling me that I had no right to this resentment — that his compulsion to turn life into words was exactly what I had come to him for in the first place.

We were infernal twins, Alex and I. We operated a Mutual Forgiveness Bureau with ourselves as the exclusive clients. Our symbiosis was precisely balanced — I got depressed for him; he became euphoric for me. A perfect working relation-ship. All excesses were forgiven, all vulgarities. You scratch the skin off my back, I'll scratch the skin off yours. How well we understood each other. Our collusions were the glue which bound us together.

The trade-offs (a partial list):

Your infidelities for my hysterics.
Your genius for my little-girlishness.
Your female-mania for my domomania.
Your prophethood for my dilettantism.

It was a fragile and sometimes wobbly balance which we were constantly adjusting. We juggled, we discarded, we added, we divided. The one process we avoided, by tacit consent, was multiplication. That, we both suspected, would throw a spanner into the delicate and complex construction of our lego-lives. We were a tightly closed two-man system. There was no room for outsiders.

But it happened, as it inevitably does — pills, diaphragms, telephonus interruptus notwithstanding. Multiplication. The one unknown quantity in our perfectly worked-out equation. A tiny little comma of flesh inside me that was going to grow into a sentence a paragraph, a chapter, a whole book. . . .

Except that it didn't. It was a full stop. The only thing it did was to send out red ink blots — tell-tale stains which sent a shiver of dread through me now that I'd made up my mind to the fact of pregnancy. I developed the world's best vocabulary with which to describe to the doctor the various hues and consistencies of those stains — rusty, grainy, clotted, scarlet, pink, watery, crimson, vermilion. Each minor variation, it seemed, was of prime importance to the receptive and knowing eye of my gynecologist.

"Spotting," pronounced the doctor. "Relax. Stay in bed. Don't engage in sexual intercourse."

"Yes, Doctor, but can I *fuck*?"

I went to bed. So did Alex — to Hella's bed and to Christine's bed and to Gina's bed and to Faye's bed. The one I occupied was somehow too much like a hospital cot. I found a new vocation in life — I became a Spot Examiner. A swift swoop of the Kleenex between the legs. Dare I look? What would it be? What unpredictable changes would my disloyal uterus ring on the colour spectrum this time? An ecstatic flutter of the heart if the dampness turned out to be a lovely neutral nothingness; a distressingly painful pang if there was a trace of blood, even a pinkish tinge. A visit to the toilet was like going over the trench top.

Alex existed only as a medium for keeping the neck of my uterus tightly shut or causing it to flutter open. For once I felt I was doing something more important than Alex. Or, if that was too excessive a statement, something just as important. I'd moved out of his orbit. Suddenly he became *my* construct. Role reversal of the most unsavoury kind. He quickly sensed that he'd been reduced to the role of spectator in this latest little drama.

In an effort to recapture centre stage, his behaviour became more and more outrageous. He never came home before three or four in the morning. The phone jangled constantly with urgent female messages. A silent unacknowledged tussle went on between us. How long was I going to be able to maintain my separateness? Me and It versus Him. We were locked in combat but this time it was not a complementary combat. Something or someone else had added rules which had nothing to do with the psychic survival of either of us. Insofar as Alex was becoming aware of this X factor, he was frightened and appalled. Insofar as I was becoming aware of it, I was frightened and elated.

The spotting stopped for days on end. The doctor told me I could now get out of bed but I had to continue to be both celibate and cautious. I knew that quitting bed meant entering the old familiar arena, the one in which I was constantly getting trounced. For the first time in my life with Alex, I refused to take up the challenge, refused to clamber back inside the ropes. For the first time I wanted not in, but out. Only for a few days, mind. But I recognized that something was beginning to change.

Too cowardly to tell my doctor, I sneakily did it anyway — I flew to New York again to stay with Rosie. Rosie shared a cold-water flat on East 11th Street with 150 million cockroaches and 8 billion black fleas. The rest of the space was taken up by Mickey Mice. Plastic Mickies, tin Mickies, papier-mâché Mickies, cast-iron Mickies. They varied in size from six inches to six feet. Minnie was conspicuous by her absence. Mounds of empty Count Chocula cereal boxes lay strewn over the floor. They had been emptied, not by the cockroaches, but by Rosie.

Rosie was immensely fat but she was also immensely beautiful. Somehow, her size enhanced her beauty. She was like an overgrown Botticelli. Her eyes looked as if they'd just come from adoring the Christ child; her mouth, as if it had just finished giving King Kong a blow job. She carried on an animated conversation with me while she typed her weekly column for a large Sydney newspaper — her fingers didn't seem to need the attention of her mind. If she could've typed with her toes, she'd no doubt have written a novel at the same time.

"What's with you and this Alex character?" she asked me. "And don't give me any shit — you didn't look happy last time you came down here, and you don't look happy now. Come clean, kid!"

But that was the last thing in the world I was able to do. Alex and I belonged to a cabal that restricted its members to two. Not even Rosie was allowed to visit.

Besides, I hadn't come to New York to talk, as I reminded her. I had come to buy maternity clothes. Dozens and dozens of them. Another bit of primitive magic — if I bought maternity clothes I'd have to expand to fill them.

Rosie accompanied me on my shopping missions. She knew maternity departments well — they were the only places where she could find clothes to fit her.

In the dressing room, knee high in caftans and kangaroo-pouched slacks, I was suddenly seized by nauseatingly familiar contractions. I doubled up on the stack of clothes, a rush of warm wetness between my legs. Cautiously I raised myself up from the place where I lay. I could tell from the expression on Rosie's face what I was going to see even before I saw it — a spreading pool of bright-red blood on the beige print of a maternity smock. I refused to acknowledge it. The maternity department of Bloomingdale's was not where you had a miscarriage. I picked myself up and continued to try on things.

Rosie had already mobilized shop assistants and a taxi, but I refused to leave until I'd made at least one purchase. Luckily, Rosie was crazy enough herself to recognize craziness in others — even to respect it — so we spent an extra five

189

minutes in the fitting room arguing passionately about the respective merits of a purple-patterned jacket or a lolly-pink smock dress. By the time we had decided on the jacket ("You can always wear it afterwards," hinted Rosie gently) I was dribbling blood all over the floor of Bloomingdale's, and even the hardened street-wise New Yorkers were beginning to stare.

Back on the black leather table. My home away from home. A white-robed nun was bending over me, fiddling with something above my head. The back of my gown was soaked with blood, the front with tears.

"It's all right, dear," said the emergency-room nun in unctuous tones of infinite compassion and forbearance, "you'll be over it in no time."

"How the fuck would you know?" I said, thinking, You sterile old cunt. I was amazed and horrified at my viciousness. The expression on the nun's face didn't change. Nor did she flinch. She was used to it. The syphilitics, the drug-crazed addicts, the women with half their wombs ripped out with knitting needles, the drunks with their heads split open — the detritus coming off the streets of New York. Compared to them, I was merely a respectable little hausfrau having a respectable little miscarriage.

I swam up from under the swampy sea of anesthesia. Rosie was there beside my bed. She saw me opening my eyes and held out the purple maternity jacket. It was festooned all over with dozens of grinning Mickey Mouse badges. "That's for the next time you're pregnant," she said. "Don't take off a single badge or you'll end up here again with all the white-robed spookies."

A nun bore down on me with a giant syringe. She ordered me to lie on my side and bare my buttocks for the plunge. Before Rosie disappeared behind the screen she murmured to me, deliberately loud enough for the sister to hear, "Don't forget to turn the other cheek, darling." But not even that could muster a smile from me. I felt like a spook myself, grey and formless and utterly devoid of substance.

"What hospital am I in?" I asked Rosie.

"St. Vincent's," she answered, and then added as an afterthought, "Actually, you've probably heard of it. It's the one Dylan Thomas died in."

I jerked upright, my eyes wide open. "This very hospital?"

"Well, yes," said Rosie. "Probably right on the floor above."

For the first time since my miscarriage I broke into a radiant smile; a burst of energy jolted through me like an electric bolt. I started waving my arms around like a maniac. "Dylan Thomas died here? Right here where I am? *He* was here?"

Suddenly everything was all right, part of a master plan I could understand and feel at home with.

Rosie looked at my smiling face, my bright eyes, my gesticulating arms. "So what?" she asked, genuinely puzzled. "What has that to do with what's happening to you?"

I stared at her and realized that she didn't have a clue, that my dear crazy Rosie was a complete stranger.

As soon as she left the ward, I hobbled to the phone to call Alex in Montreal. I couldn't wait to tell him that I was having a miscarriage on the very spot where Dylan had breathed his last. This was something only he'd understand.

That night I dreamt I'd given birth to a thin little rectangular fishcake. I placed it carefully on my bedside table and when I awoke I felt so hungry I gobbled it down. The minute I had swallowed the last fishy morsel, a sharp pang of horror stabbed through me. I had eaten my own baby! My own baby was in the process of being turned into shit. . . . I woke up in a cold sweat.

The Typewriter in the Bath

How do I ruin thee? Let me count the ways. . . . My domomania being for the moment satisfied, uteromania took over. Although Alex and I were each other's perfect filling machines, he revolted against the primitivism of being reduced to a breeding machine; the pleasure dome being turned into a unionized factory. It was a reaction I understood, as I understood all of Alex's reactions. But it didn't stop me in my own ruthless drives. We were bulldozers, both of us, except that Alex had the bad luck to look like one. . . .

My mother moved from her old Bellevue Hill flat, with all its memories, to a "nice little unit" in Bondi Junction. When she wrote me about this, she also included a photo of my father's grave. My name was engraved on the gravestone. I felt a surge of anger at having it there, inscribed for every passing mourner to read. It made me feel violated, bound to my father's body for all eternity.

The same letter brought other disturbing news. Fanya, at her doctor's insistence, had been examined and found to have cancer in her left breast. The offending breast had been removed, scooped out. That foul sickness, the great family heirloom, had struck again.

It gave me a strange feeling to imagine my mother in surroundings that had nothing to do with me.

Her body had changed; so had her house. It was as if she had gotten a divorce without asking my permission.

Scene: We're having a dinner party. Seven guests are sitting around our dining-room table. A couple of editors, CBC directors, two unknown poets, one well-known novelist. There is a small knot of tension in my stomach. Will the conversation be allowed to flow as happily and easily as it's going? Or will Alex start raving about the daily murders of marriage, about the necessity of freedom for the artist, about Woman the Castrator?

I serve up the Vichyssoise. Delicious. Everyone compliments me. Then the Coquilles St. Jacques. Aren't I a grand little cook? A grand little companion? A grand little lay? I breathe a sigh of relief — we've made it through to the Strawberries Romanov. But only just. One bite of his rum-drenched strawberry and Alex takes off like a supersonic jet. Vr-oo-oo-m! Up, up and away! "Marriage!" he shouts. "Marriage is a snore and a delusion, a Venus fly trap for the unwary. . . ."

If it wasn't for the crushing, numbing responsibility of marriage, he, Alex, would spread his gossamer wings and fly through the world. He'd be a monk in that monastery high up on Mount Athos where no woman is allowed to enter. Not even animals are allowed, in case they're female. Those Greek monks have the right idea, by god.

Where do I look? More to the point, where do our guests look?

We all end up staring into our dessert dishes until Alex winds down his diatribe and the evening can once again resume its amiability. "Coffee, little one," he bellows. "Coffee for all of us, and some of that scrumptious cherry strudel you made this afternoon. We don't want our guests to leave the table feeling hungry, do we?"

No, Alex. We certainly don't. No.

The next time around it took. Something real came to live inside me at last. I could feel my empty spaces filling up. I jumped onto the examination table, stuck my legs up in the stirrups like the good little gynecological athlete I had become and submitted yet again to the gloved, probing finger. A look of grave concentration on God the Doctor's face. He who Giveth and He who Taketh away. This afternoon he's giving. I'm pregnant and in great shape.

I sailed through the first three months like a ship on course. I was as spotless as Maria Immaculata. Kleenex tissues came away from between my legs in their original rainbow-hued colours, untainted by any tear-away membranes. My pants were the cleanest and whitest in town. My swollen breasts were huge, my nipples sore and prickly. My belly began to shove out ever so slightly against my skirt.

For one whole morning I entertained the thought that the evil inheritance of Monny's chin had skipped a generation only to be visited on the unfortunate one now inside me. I even imagined I could see the tip of a monstrous chin poking out of my belly mound. But I forced myself to dispel such morbid Fanya-like fantasies.

Alex retreated before the reality of the growing pregnancy — its autonomy shoved him into an increasingly smaller space. I saw myself growing more and more real; Alex saw me growing more and more abstract. Our carefully-worked-out construction began to develop an ungainly lopsided bulge. To bring it back into line, Alex grafted more pieces onto his side; carpeted his space with wall-to-wall ladies. Wherever Alex went, they went too, blackbirds in his already bursting pie.

The King was in the counting house
   counting out his pomes;
The Queen was in the parlour
   eating shit and bones.

King Alex was getting richer and richer; Queen Anna was getting sicker and sicker.

Scene: "I've been working damn hard," announces Alex cheerfully. "This teaching is drying me up, sapping my energies. My publisher is sending me on a cross-country reading tour. Be away for about a month. Isn't it great? A tour like this is a major breakthrough for me. Next stop, Stockholm!"

The tour means that Alex will be away for all of Christmas and New Year. That I'll be alone. Alone and pregnant. Don't go, Alex, I want to say. I need you here. They can do the reading tour without you. They can get someone else. It doesn't have to be *you.*

But of course it does, so I keep my subversive thoughts to myself, bow my head in martyred silence and submit to the tyrannies of both Fate and Genius.

I went to the airport to wave good-bye. A pathetic slightly swollen little lady. St. Anna of the Perpetual Sorrows. An icon of abandonment and despair. But this time the role didn't quite fit. Somehow it felt wrong. Obscene.

When I got back home, the emptiness of the house accosted me. I should have felt sorry for myself — Alex was gone, it was Christmastime, and I was a pregnant, abandoned wife. The perfect set-up for misery. But my heart wasn't in it. No matter how hard I tried, I couldn't get a kick out of it anymore. The edge was off. I felt myself moving into new territory.

I was invited to a New Year's Eve party. For the first time I dressed up in a maternity outfit. The wine-coloured dress was soft and velvety and graceful. I felt beautiful. But as I struggled to pull my boots on, a feeling of utter helplessness invaded me. It was as if I had been struck by dropsy. I couldn't propel myself through the front door — there seemed to be a force-field preventing me from leaving. I sat down on the floor, too lethargic to move. I was waiting for something to happen. For what, I hadn't the faintest notion. . . .

At two minutes to midnight, the telephone jangled. It was the signal I had been waiting for to release me from my spell. The dropsy fell from me and I sprang across the room to grab the receiver. I heard the characteristic click of the long-distance call, then the operator's voice clanged along the wires, splitting my eardrum with its tinny Australian vowels. "Mrs. Jacobs? Long distance from Sydney."

It was Uncle Jack. "Sweetheart? Is that my girl?" A sudden vivid flash of memory pulsed through me — I saw myself waking up on the couch in Jack and Bashka's flat, sunshine splashing into the room and Jack's cheerful voice calling out "Rise and shine, rise and shine!"

But Uncle Jack hadn't called long distance to tell me to rise and shine. A warning bell went off in my head. "It's so hard to tell you this, Annale. Fanya died last night. I've been trying to get through to you but all the lines have been busy. . . . Anna? Anna? Do you hear me, my dear? You must come home for the funeral. . . . We won't have it till you arrive. Anna, dear girl, for God's sake, say something."

But I couldn't open my mouth. I clenched the receiver tight in my fist. A record clicked on inside my head, the needle locked into the same groove. "This is what I was waiting for," it repeated over and over and over again.

"This is what I was waiting for. This is what I was waiting for. This is what I was waiting for. . . . "

———◇———

Two Thoughts Immediately Following News of My Mother's Death

First thought: You bitch! Your timing's perfect. Now you've fucked up New Year's Eve for the rest of my life.

Second thought: Thank bloody Christ Tom's dead. Otherwise I'd never dare go home for the funeral.

And then an avalanche of pain took over, drowning out everything else. . . .

I couldn't reach out to Alex for help. He wasn't there. I had only myself, Fanya's daughter, and this other strange self, Fanya's grandchild, who lay coiled up inside me, unaware that it had just lost its last chance — for better or for worse — of having a grandparent. I realized for the first time that "only myself" would have to be enough.

I lie down on the bed, still in coat and boots, and think of the journey ahead. A click in the lock. The stealthy turn of the key. Familiar footsteps towards the bedroom. Alex is back. When he should have been hundreds of miles away. Pad, pad, down the hall.

"Where's my wife? Where's my preggy little wifey?" He rounds the corner of the darkened bedroom. "Blizzards! Snowstorms! Winds! No audiences! What idiots would arrange a tour at this time! What shmucks! And anyway — " a tactical afterthought — "couldn't let my little one stay by herself on New Year's Eve, could I?"

He pauses at the bedroom door and looks over at me, baffled. Why wasn't I jumping up to hug him in joy, in gratitude, for the splendid gift of his presence?

Instead, I sit up in bed and say in a strangled voice, "My mother's dead. I'm going. Leaving. Me and the baby. Fanya's dead."

My bag is packed. I lie on the bed, staring into the dark. Alex has been up all night typing. Tap, tap, click. Tap, tap, click. Tap, tap, click. . .choong. Tap, click, tap tap tap. . . choong. When I get up at dawn, I see the typewriter sitting in the middle of Alex's desk, sticking a long, white tongue out at me — "Elegy for Fanya" is written on its tip.

I don't bother to read all the stuff underneath. Instead, I go into the bathroom and run a bath. A pleasantly warm bath into which I shake some nice-smelling crystals. Then I go back into the study, lift the typewriter off the desk, carry it into the bathroom, put it in the bath and drown it. I hold it under the water until I can feel that it has stopped twitching and that, at long last, it is still.

It's January the first. The world has started up again. I phone my doctor from the airport to tell him that I'm going to Australia. He warns me of the foolhardiness of undertaking such an exhausting journey. "I'd be irresponsible if I didn't warn you, Mrs. Jacobs, that the fifth month is a highly vulnerable time. Especially with your history."

Fuck my history! Fuck my vulnerability! If whoever was in me couldn't hold fast on such an occasion, if it was disloyal enough to desert me just when I needed it most, then let it. It had to have some sort of responsibility towards me, too. I was taking it to bury its grandmother. I was flying off and away and it had better hang on in there if it wanted to keep up with me. . . .

Part III

Stop Shovelling

The perfumed humid shimmering heat of Sydney, its haze of pollen dust hanging almost static in the heavy air. And the light — that trumpeting bugle-burst of light that hits clean between the eyes like a golden bullet. The juicy jungle greenness of oleanders, gardenias, jasmine, frangipanis. The unbearably heavy sweetness of odours which puff out in soft intense bursts. The clotted creaminess of the blossoms; the head-invading hysteria of the cicada thrum. And, falling through the tangle of tall trees, deep dappled pools of sunshine into which darting birds, like animated jewels, dip their wings. Australia. Bush. Beach. Jungle. Desert. Home. The arctic wastes of Montreal left behind, forgotten as if they had never existed.

My surviving family is gathered around Sonya's table which is piled high with mangoes, plums, pawpaws, passionfruit. I note how strangely their pale sad faces go with the pagan gaudiness of the fruit. My aunts are no longer my aunts. They're passionately disappointed women, the ghosts of excited girls, hopeful wives, tender mothers trembling in their eyes.

Bashka and Jack now have three "little nippers," three beautiful dark-eyed daughters who will no doubt grow up expecting the world to be a recreation of the loving, gentle atmosphere of their home.

But Bashka's face is ploughed with deep furrows of anxiety — her husband's idealism has eroded into impotence but he refuses to recognize this. He insists on hanging onto his failing bookstore with an optimism that borders on obstinacy.

My Aunty Sonya's obsession with Misha's musical gift has pitched her into a high, humming neurasthenia. Her voice whines like a tuning fork. Not that she hasn't cause enough for nervousness. Misha, although only in his sixties, has been ravaged by the onset of premature senility. He still manages to carry on his teaching, but his hands shake and his eyes blink. It's obvious his wife's single-minded devotion is beginning to arouse in him a large and boundless fury. Jessica, my ten-year-old cousin, confides in me with subdued gleeful giggles that he is constantly flicking the ashes of his foul-smelling cigarettes onto Aunty Sonya's head — he thinks it's an ashtray. When he comes to the end of his cigarette, he has to be restrained from stubbing it out onto her scalp. Uncle Misha is a heavy smoker, and I've already had many opportunities to observe this strange phenomenon.

"Crikey," quavers my bad-boy uncle, "strike me pink! What's wrong, eh? What's all the fuss about, eh?"

"The ashtray!" shrieks the outraged Sonya. Then, recalling herself, "Be a pet, Mishale. Use the ashtray."

My family has split open like an overripe melon. As I watch them, my aunts seem to uncoil themselves like wraiths of smoke from where they have been hiding all the years of my life — from under my armpits, behind my ears, in between my toes — and reassemble themselves into solid chunks of flesh. They are finally who they are. Themselves. Apart. To be taken into some sort of account as separate bodies who exist outside my own fantastical head.

And what of my mother who sits, like Banquo's ghost, shaking her gory locks at me from a chair across the table? Can I finally manage to uncoil her from me? See her at last as her own self? For the first time since hearing of her death,

I visualize Fanya in her plain wooden box. The flesh is just beginning to putrefy, sinking like grey-pink sludge into the jagged hole on the left side of her chest. I can catch a whiff of the sickly-sweet stench insinuating itself from under the coffin lid. It makes straight for me, trying to fray the edges of *my* flesh, trying to pull me into the clammy breast hole. But it stops before it touches me. Just in time.

My mother is shut tight in the box, nailed down in her coffin. I'm here. Breathing. Sweating. With an embryo inside me pulsating with the energy of multiplying cells. We are, finally, Fanya and I, separate beings. Me and my mother. My mother. Me.

Fanya is to be buried at ten o'clock tomorrow morning. Tonight — my mother's last night above ground — I'm supposed to relax, have a light, nourishing supper, take a shower, go to bed early. I have, after all, "someone else to think of now." And surely I must be exhausted, drained, jet-lagged, grief-stricken. I am, I am. I'm all of these things. But I'm also exhilarated, energized, excited. Something is happening inside my head.

I perpetrate my first act of disobedience. No, I shan't go to bed early. No, I shan't relax. Instead, shutting myself into the guest room to escape the vigilant eyes — Fanya's eyes — of my aunts, I look up Patrick Sullivan's number and call him. I give him my aunt's Bellevue Hill address and ask him to pick me up.

We fuck all through the prickly blanket heat of the sweltering Sydney night. Gorgeous releasing fucks. I'm not scared that I'm going to have a miscarriage — I'm coming hard and often but I'm not scared. Whoever's in there is going to have to hang on to the riggings. Survive a rough stormy night on the Amniotic Sea. Withstand the giant sea-snake attacks of Patrick's prick. And it will. This time I'm convinced I have a faithful ally inside me. A fully committed passenger who's going to finish the journey with me instead of bailing out halfway through.

I wake up to a sun-splashed room. Patrick has thrown open the shutters and through the leaves of the frangipani tree outside his window I can see the hard-diamond glitter of the harbour, can hear the morning shrieks of the cockatoos — all the joyous harsh and brassy sounds of a Sydney summer morning.

The heat vibrates with an electric twang. We hose each other down with ice-cold water in the wild overgrown bamboo garden of Patrick's courtyard and feast on passionfruit and pawpaws. Then I jump into his white jeep and he drives me through the funky iron-balustraded dollhouses of Paddington to the sober burghers' houses of Bellevue Hill.

On this day I am going to bury my mother.

The sleek black funeral cars purr as they drive out through the ugly broiling suburbs. I avert my eyes from the sodden faces of my aunts and stare out the car windows at the women in their gaudy sundresses, string bags bulging with morning shopping, their painted faces toughened to the consistency of leather. The men, buttocky in their laundered shorts, rush by like prime herds of beef on the hoof. We've left behind the lush harboured splendour of the Eastern Suburbs and are traversing the sterile wastes of the West towards Rookwood (could Shakespeare have chosen a better name?), the Suburb of the Dead, the largest Jewish ghetto in the Southern Hemisphere. The final in-gathering of the farthest-flung of the diaspora. Here is where they all come home to roost and this is where my family lives — my great-grand-mother, my grandmother, my grandfather, my Aunty Milly, my father. In this quiet haven, all Jews lie together in the enforced neutrality of death — the snotty culture-vulture Germans, the despised Galizianers, thick-headed Roumanians, vulgar grasping Polacks, simple-minded Litvacks, and the generous, intelligent, idealistic Russians to which group, needless to say, my own family belongs.

The cars weave their prissy self-important way through the numbered streets of the necropolis. We stop before an open grave — my mother's new one-bedroom apartment where the borders will always be full of dust and where she won't be able to do a damn thing about it.

The sweaty brick-faced grave-diggers standing at mock-humble attention behind the mound of freshly dug earth. The pine coffin (is it possible that Fanya, my mother, lies so quietly, so uncomplainingly, behind that fragile lid?). The knot of black-clad men. The huddled blob of weeping women. The classic simplicity of the death ritual — an ancient Greek drama being played out in an Australian suburb.

Someone shoves me gently towards the chorus of female weepers, but I refuse to be drawn into the intimacy of their communal grief. I stand apart. Alone. I don't want to be touched.

Rabbi Bernstein starts the service. He throws me a disapproving look. His fleshy pastoral nose has already sniffed me out as the Infidel, the one who refuses to join his servile snuffling woolly flock. I resent his too-healthy appearance. He looks as if he has been surfeited on feeding and fucking, and I remember my childhood shame that rabbis never looked as properly consumptive as priests and ministers, whose long mean faces seemed so much more in keeping with the dignity of their profession.

The self-conscious nasal resonances of Rabbi Bernstein's unctuous patronizing sermon in the Chevra Kadisha has, he suspects, pissed me off — ". . . her loving daughter Anna, who, forsaking husband, home and the demands of her teaching career, has made the long journey across the ocean to be here today with her sorrowing family on this, the tragic occasion of her beloved mother's untimely death. . . ."

Fuck you, Rabbi! Don't think the dramatic mysteries of your curly black beard can hide your pursy fat overfed mouth from me! This funeral is bad street theatre. I want nothing to do with it.

Until I hear him intoning, *"Yisgadal, v'yiskadash sh'may rebbo. . . . "* Involuntarily, automatically, I start moving away. I'm a little girl again in the synagogue at Yom Kippur and the grave-faced adults are pushing me and all the other children out of the *shul*. We who are not bereaved must not have our ears contaminated by the chant of mourning. I remember sneaking to the side window and spying on the adult rituals that were being practised in secrecy — the cries, the muffled wails and, over the noise of a weeping congregation, the solemn sonorities of *"Yisgadal, v'yiskadash. . . "*

With a thudding jolt I realize that now I'm a legitimate mourner, that no longer can I claim immunity. That it's *my* mother who has died; *my* father who lies buried not too many plots away; that now I'm the one who stands on the front line.

For the first time in my life, I am nobody's daughter.

The dull thud of earth hitting wood. Each man of the *minyan* moves forward and shovels one clod of soil onto the coffin lid. After that, the chief mourners among the women will throw a handful onto the grave and then the whole party will move away from the plot and let the gravediggers proceed with the real burial.

Since my mother had no brothers, Alex would have shovelled the first clod. For the first time since I arrived I want him to be here. In his absence Uncle Jack steps forward. Tears streaming down his face, he digs his shovel into the dry, crumbly orange-yellow soil. Clop! The hollow finality of soil on wood. After him come Uncle Misha and Uncle Srulik. Uncle Srulik is not, strictly speaking, my uncle but merely the brother of a great-uncle by marriage. He has remained a bachelor for all of his seventy-eight years, and for the past few years has become more and more passive — he goes through the motions of living only at the behest of others.

Today he has been ordered to bury his brother's niece. A quick turn of the invisible wooden key in his back and he moves forward, bends from the waist like a toy soldier, thrusts in the shovel, tosses the soil. But something has gone wrong with his mechanism. Poor Srulik thinks he's a Perpetual Motion machine. Instead of stepping back into the respectable anonymity of the *minyan*, he's off again, a military step forward, a sharp thrust into the soil, a smart toss into the grave. Scoop, toss. Scoop, toss. Scoop, toss.

Everyone freezes. Tragedy is being turned into farce. Unless somebody does something, Srulik is going to scoop and toss, scoop and toss, for all eternity. Luckily, my Aunty Sonya comes to the rescue. "Srulik! Stop shovelling!" Srulik looks timidly over his shoulder at my aunt. She glares back at him. "Stop shovelling already!"

Srulik drops his head. He knows that he has been a naughty boy. Hangdog, he drops the spade and shuffles back into the protective huddle of the *minyan*. More men step forward. The clods of soil thwack onto my mother. She is being planted deep and firm into Australian soil. She's part of Australia now, just as my father is and my grandfather and my aunt. Accepted by this alien island in death as they never were in life. At home, finally.

Rabbi Bernstein is shooing everybody away from the graveside, especially my aunts and me. We're the chief mourners and must turn our faces away from death and back to life faster than anybody else. I'm damned, though, if I'm going to give in to what amounts to bullying on the part of the rabbi. I want to stand by my mother's grave alone. Just she and I and the one yet unborn.

I pretend to walk meekly towards the waiting line of cars, but then, at the last moment, I wheel back for a last look. I can hear my mother's friends whispering noisily behind me. "Poor girl. Wants one more look at Fanya . . . could've made more visits while she was alive." Twitter, twitter.

There is a huge lump in my chest. It won't dissolve. My eyes are like two stones, dead and dry. Not even Moses could strike water out of them.

The grave is practically filled in. I look at the layer of dry rubbly soil and have to remind myself who lies beneath. I keep telling myself that it is my mother. Telling myself that I am attending my mother's funeral, that I'll never be able to say "mother" to anyone again as long as I live, that her smells, her voice, her hair, her fingernails, are dead. The whole jumbled confusion of our connection is over. Forever.

And finally my stoniness begins to dissolve and great blobs of warm tears fall from my eyes. I'm melting, liquefying. My nipples sting and tingle and it seems as if heavy sweet gushes of milk are throbbing out onto my blouse and spilling down over my belly. And between my legs, on the inside of my thighs, I can feel Patrick's semen trickling down in warm pearly tickly-sticky drops. Past my knees, over my ankles, onto the dry soil.

I'm streaming liquid from head to toe — tears and sweat and nose-run and mouth-dribble and milk and come. All running in an endless flow from my body into the grave dirt. It soaks right through the loose layer of topsoil on my mother's grave, through the cracks in her coffin, and pours into the gaping hole where her left breast used to be, filling it up with wet and warmth. Into her dried yellow and mauve eye sockets, into her cracked and blackened mouth, into the rotting cavities of her decaying nose. My milk feeding my mother.

The syrupy liquids flood all through the cemetery, moistening and softening the drought-hardened soil of Rookwood. Into my grandfather's lung cavity; into my great-grandmother's eye socket; into the dark deep hollow of Aunty Milly's caved-in chest. Lushness. Wetness. Filling all the holes. Overflowing. . . .

Somebody — Bashka, I think — takes me gently by the arm and leads me back to the waiting car.

A family scandal. The loving daughter, who journeyed across the ocean to attend her mother's funeral, refuses to sit *shiva*. Instead, as soon as the funeral is over, Patrick picks me up and drives me to his newly acquired property near Kurrajong. It's deep in the bush with only a rough narrow path leading into it. There's a tent and a lean-to and an open stone fireplace on which we make fires out of eucalyptus branches and brew billy tea to revive us in between our love-making. We fuck everywhere — underneath the casuarinas where willy wagtails spy on us and call us "sweet pretty creatures, sweet pretty creatures"; in the oily heat of the tent; on the prickly dry grass of a clearing miles away from the campsite where a raggy, remote moon shines down on us and the fluorescent white bark of the ghost-gums shimmers in the night.

A vision in the bush: Patrick has gone to inspect the fences bounding his property. I sit on a rock at the campsite overlooking a valley. I feel an overwhelming sense of panic at being left alone. There's no aloneness like the aloneness of the Australian bush; no eeriness like the bush eeriness. No, not aloneness. The bush swarms with ghosts which nudge at me, invade me with an empty annihilating terror. I close my eyes against the shimmering mirage heat of the morning. I begin to hear strange sounds — the flip-flop of naked soles against bare ground. The sounds become more and more insistent. Without opening my eyes I can see, I can feel, throngs of naked *lubras* pressing themselves up against me, touching me with their black horny hands, shoving their pungent-smelling bodies up against me. They are all heavily pregnant. Their hard protuberant bellies press insistently into mine. I feel myself turning black, thick-lipped, heavy; becoming a great black pregnant *lubra*, rooted, like my dead parents, to the soil of this strange land.

My mother, it seemed, lived her life so that she would have a tidy death. Life should have expanded as she grew older — she should have sat at the top of the pyramid looking contentedly down on the ever-growing base of her family fiefdom — children, grandchildren, great-grandchildren. Except that for my mother there was only me, and she died not knowing that there was going to be more to follow. Would that have made a difference? Would the knowledge of a coming grandchild mean that her tight, tidy world would suddenly have spilled over into a warm friendly splurge of messiness?

Her Bondi Junction flat is as impersonal as a well-run motel. Not a speck of dust, not a misplaced object. Even her death was orderly. She had complained of tiredness, gone to bed early and then quietly and neatly died. Not even the sheets were wrinkled, not a hair out of place. There had been no agonized upheaval, no unruly protest. She had simply and politely ceased to exist. Her drawers and cupboards are papered and perfect; each object arranged as if placed on a pencilled outline.

Bashka and Sonya refuse to take anything beyond a few personal trinkets. I press Fanya's clothes on them — I loathe the thought of other people picking them over, of strange women I've never seen parading through the streets of Bondi Junction wearing her cardigans or skirts. I'd rather throw them out or burn them, but my aunts say it would be a crime not to give such good things to the Jewish needy.

It seemed that Fanya's one wild extravagance was her shoes. Rows and rows of them are lined up in her closet, their jaunty little shoe trees testifying to the meticulousness of their owner. I urge Bashka to try on a pair of pearl-grey suede pumps. She slips her stockinged feet into them; they fit perfectly. She takes a few tentative steps, then flings them off with a violent gesture as if her toes had hit a nest of scorpions. "They're my sister's shoes," she cries as she collapses into a chair. "I can't wear my dead sister's shoes!"

For the first time since my arrival in Sydney, we all embrace — Sonya and Bashka and myself — and cry together, my mother's discarded pumps lying forlorn in a corner of her bedroom.

There's nothing in my mother's flat to keep, nothing to quicken my memories. After my father died, did she get rid of everything that reminded her of her former life? I feel a spasm of anger. How dare she deprive me of the objects of my childhood? Not even the small things remain — the Yardley powderbox patterned with pale orange and white powder puffs; the netted velvet hats with the tiny dead birds nestling demurely inside their upturned brims; the miniature Japanese tea service; the mantel statue of Apollo and Daphne, entwined with leaves and garlands; the crystal decanters. Didn't she know, Fanya, that she was the custodian of these treasures, not the owner?

In despair I make a pilgrimage to my childhood home in Centennial Park. A pungent whiff of nostalgia overwhelms me. I haven't been back since Grandfather Zuckerman moved us to Melbourne.

But wait a minute. Something's out of focus. I'm looking through the wrong end of a telescope. The front lawn, which I had remembered as a many-acred park, has dwindled to the size of a postage stamp; the wild rose jungle at the side of the house where snot-nosed Phyllis and I sat for hours looking into flowers has been reduced to a patch of scraggly branches.

My palms are sweaty with tension as I ring the door bell. What shall I say? Will the woman of the house shut the door on me? *My* door. *My* house. I pray that no one will be home, so I may escape.

But the door opens wide on my childhood. I am welcomed by two young men who have recently bought the house. Darcy and Kevin. They make no attempt to disguise the fact that they are in love with each other. It makes me feel good. I would have hated to find some pinched-up housewife regarding me with suspicion and hostility.

As soon as I explain my visit, Darcy and Kevin pull me through the front door. Goody! They're delighted. Now I can advise them about restoring the place to its former purity. I am that rare and exotic bird, an Original Inhabitant, sent in the nick of time to rescue them from the horrors of crassness. "Here is where the toilet was — not there. Here, where you can see the tops of the trees from where you're sitting. . . . Yes, the verandah used to be open. My father had the louvres put in to turn it into my bedroom. . . . No, the fireplace never worked."

Sudden ridiculous visions of a be-slippered and be-piped Feivel stoking up a glowing coal fire, while Fanya rocks contentedly in a rush-caned chair knitting a bunny-wool pixie cap for me, her angelic-faced child, who sleeps peacefully in a wooden cradle by the open hearth.

"Yes, those twelve-o-clocks in the front garden were there right from the beginning." ("Beaut-o, Kev. Now we don't have to root the buggers out, after all.")

Our family, it appeared, had been living not in a home but in an artifact. Darcy and Kevin made me feel like the curator of a priceless museum. While answering their excited questions, I'm looking around at my own private stock of treasures. Over there is the sink where Thelma chopped off her finger; here the bath where I trailed my silvery length of Kolynos; here the cupboard of a room — now Darcy's "studio" — where Thelma slept and where I recuperated from whooping cough. Off the kitchen I can see a tiny area which some villain has spitefully shrunk from an enormous jungle to a mean, cramped backyard.

In the main bedroom stands a double bed which occupies the same space as my parents' bed. I stare at it. On this very spot Fanya and Feivel lay separately side by side, miraculously getting together on only one occasion — or so I'm convinced — to conceive me. And it was here that Feivel perpetrated his foul unnatural acts on the innocent body of his girl-child. It gladdens me that finally two people who are in love are sleeping here.

Suddenly I feel claustrophobic. I must get out — but not before they show me something I didn't know about. "Look up at the ceiling," they tell me when we're saying our good-byes in the living room. I look up. There's nothing I can see that I hadn't seen a million times before — a pukey cream plaster ceiling with a few dreary waratahs and boomerangs festering away in each corner. "We were going to plaster it over," they announce proudly. "But then we were told that it's one of the few surviving examples of Early Australiana. Now, of course, we won't touch it except to restore a few loose bits. It's a protected ceiling."

A protected ceiling! I'd spent the greater part of my childhood under a protected ceiling and hadn't even known it. . . .

------&------

Contents of Fanya's laundry hamper

(into which I surreptitiously thrust my nose to catch the last lingering whiff of mother smell)

1 hand towel (small)
4 prs. floral pants
1 bra (pink)
1 coffee-coloured half slip with off-white lace edging
2 prs. stockings (gun-metal grey)
1 cotton nightie (pale yellow)

Contents of Fanya's fridge

3 brown eggs
quarter pound of smoked roe
1 jar red horseradish sauce (almost empty)
sliver of butter
3 peaches (withered)
small carton sour cream (unused)
1 slice honey cake (carefully wrapped in grease-
    proof paper)
1 jar "Kosher-style" pickled cucumbers (half used)

Objects I throw out which make me realize that Fanya is truly dead

1 toothbrush (with a little rubber spike on the end to
    massage the gums)
1 yellow plastic comb
a partial dental plate (containing two lower back teeth)

1 salmon-pink sandbag (to be inserted on the empty side
   of a 38C bra)

I have found the only thing of value that I've been searching
for among my mother's possessions — two large caved-in
cardboard boxes full of old photos. The only untidy ill-kept
objects in the flat. The family photos stare up at me through
jumbled piles. What lies! What hypocrisy! Smiling faces, arms
draped lovingly around receptive shoulders. Fanya and Feivel
clinging to each other in a spasm of domestic bliss. He,
dandling Baby on his knees, his face loving and protective.
She, nursing drowsy, contented daughter at her breast, which
is covered, for modesty's sake, with a small towel. And
everywhere there is little Jane Powell. Smiling. Grinning.
Waving. Blue eyes shining winningly into the camera, legs
crossed prettily. Anna in an elaborately smocked dress, her
violin tucked under her chin, her bow poised delicately over
the strings. Aunts, uncles, cousins, friends — all captured
forever in a state of grinning harmony.
   I pick up the boxes and head for the bathroom. I fill my
mother's rose-coloured bath with tepid water. One of Fanya's
black pubic hairs floats to the surface. It looks alive —
springy and sexual. Is that how my mother's cunt felt? My
mind slithers away from the thought of her black sprouting
hole. Rather than touch the hair, I drain the bath and start
filling it up all over again.
   Carefully I empty the cartons of photos into the water.
They float on the surface, jostling one another.
   I notice a photo of my Aunty Milly sitting on a horse.
She is wearing cream-coloured jodhpurs and what looks like
a very expensive beautifully cut silk shirt. She sits up straight
on the horse, her smartly booted legs stuck firmly into the
stirrups, her hands lightly holding the reins. And she smiles
into the camera, a confident, sporty girl out for a brisk
morning canter. Her chest hole is nowhere in evidence.
Bobbing around next to her is Anna, smiling her Kolynos

smile, twinkling away like a Walt Disney fireworks display.

Taking the toilet brush which stands in the corner ("so clean you could eat off it") I savagely jab the photos under the water. I stir and poke and splosh. Push them under until they begin to blur and soften. They're images of images. Shadows of shadows of shadows.

A picture flashes into my head — Alex and Fanya are sitting at either end of the bathtub. My mother's slack white legs are tucked inside Alex's squat hairy ones. Gog and Magog. Alex's typewriter floats in front of him and he's hunched over, typing. With each tap of the keys, a photo jumps out of the typewriter and floats towards Fanya who is smiling a blank idiot's smile. The bath is clogged with photos but still Alex does not stop tapping them out. And still my mother keeps baring her teeth in that idiotic smile. . . .

—⤜◆⤛—

Things I Find Out About Fanya Before Going Home

That she was hideously extravagant and had ruined my
father.

That she was the most generous and loving woman who
gave unstintingly of her energies and emotions to those
who were in need of it.

That she was the closest and most loyal friend to at least
five women, all of whom were heartbroken at her death.

That she had had a notorious love affair with a married
man shortly after I had left home. He had begged her
to leave Feivel, but although she loved this man, she
refused.

That she was extremely stupid.

That she was extremely intelligent.

That she cared only about herself.

That she cared only about me.

216

That my father had been passionately in love with my
mother's eldest sister, the beauteous Sonya, who had
rejected him in favour of Misha. Instead, he married
Fanya, the Ugly Sister. Fanya knew this and he knew
that she knew.

That she loved me.

That she hated me.

Who was Fanya? What was She?

Hard Questions.
Harder Answers.

I had arrived in Sydney for my mother's funeral looking pallid, sick, grey-skinned.

Three weeks later I get off the plane in Montreal, tanned, glowing, my belly large and firm. I look — and feel — obscenely healthy. Bursting with energy and optimism and an enormous sense of liberation. I feel as if I'm in a sunny field with no fences. I can gallop, kick up my heels, whinny and neigh, toss my mane and paw the ground without restraint.

I don't *have* to do anything. I don't have to love. I don't have to hate. I don't have to stay. I don't have to leave. I don't have to fuck. I don't have to *not* fuck. I'm giddy with freedom. And panic-stricken. Because I know that I have come back to Montreal to leave Alex.

It's a foregone conclusion which seems to have nothing to do with me. I toy with the idea that if it were within my power to reverse the decision, I would. I feel like someone in a science-fiction movie, where the heroine, captured by an alien from outer space, becomes the creature of another's will.

Except that after a while I realize that this is a cop-out. *I* am my own creature. *I* am the alien from outer space. It's *my* will I'm obeying, I who am in possession of myself. I no longer have to be a magic thief.

I am going to leave Alex.

The house smells of Hella's perfume. There are hair clips in the sheets, stockings under the bed, lipstick stains on the unwashed glasses. A half-empty bottle of expensive moisturizer stands in the bathroom cabinet. I use it. I feel strange. I feel wonderful.

"Little one, you look wonderful!" shouts my husband. He looks at me for a response. I say nothing.

"Look at your big fat belly and your boobies all milky and silky and soft."

No response. Alex shoots me a shrewd look and decides to play his best card.

"Let me read you a real masterpiece. I've done the best writing I've ever done since you've been away. I've even written a poem for our baba. . . . "

Silence.

Alex sniffs danger. He stops prancing around the room, stops riffling through his papers. He looks caged and cagey.

"Guess what? While you were away I was appointed poet-in-residence at U. of T. We're moving to Toronto. . . You want to live in Toronto, don't you?

"It'll be a new start for the two of us — for the three of us."

I open my mouth for the first time. "It's too late, Alex."

"This time we'll get a dream house, a charmer. All our friends will envy us."

"Too late!" I shout. "Too late!" I break into a clammy sweat. My throat feels like a rough piece of knotted rope. "It's too late! *Too fucking late!*"

Alex is going to Toronto as soon as the term finishes. With or without Hella. It's no longer my concern. It's no longer my pain. I shall stay on in the house until the baby is born and then I shall think about where I'm going to live and what I'm going to do with the large new chunk of life I've given myself for a present. We inhabit separate bedrooms until Alex can find another place.

I'm awakened from a restless sleep by a banging from the spare bedroom. It's 2:00 A.M. Sounds of dry rasping sobs. Dull thudding sound of flesh on plaster. I go in. Alex is sitting up in bed wailing, bashing his head against the wall.

I feel as if someone has bored holes in the soles of my feet and my body organs have dropped through. The pain of Alex's pain is unbearable. I want him to sing, to shout, to recite poetry — anything, rather than reveal his agony. One word from me — one magical word — and he will be healed. Now I have that power. I can reverse everything that I have set in motion. I have only to utter one small word and it'll all be as it was before. Just one unhinging of the jaw, one movement of the lips, of the tongue. I clamp my mouth shut, press my teeth together until I can feel my jaw ache.

I refuse to betray myself, but I cannot turn my back on him. I get into his bed.

"This isn't what I want," he moans. "Don't leave me. I don't want you to." His mouth goes straight down on my nipple, nuzzling and worrying at it like a hungry baby. His cock hardens, slips between my thighs. "Don't go. It isn't what I want," he moans.

I look down at him — his mouth at my nipple like a child's, his cock between my legs like my father's. It all seems wrong. Terribly, terribly wrong.

"This isn't what I want," he moans again.

All of a sudden I find the words that won't betray me. They're so simple and ordinary I can't understand why I've never used them before. "No," I say quietly, moving away. "It's what *I* want."

Sample Dialogue from My Last Days with Alex

Sample one:

"But I love you."
"Yes, I know."
"But you love me."
"Yes, I know."
"So why are you doing this terrible thing?"
"Because I love you."
Because we're each other's child. Because we're each other's parents. Because I'm your mother. Because I'm your daughter. Because somehow in the infernal workings of our marriage, I've missed out on being your wife.

Sample two:

"I can't live alone. I need you."
"Go live with Hella."
"I can't."
"Why?"
"Because her breasts are like fried eggs."
"Eat them."
"Because she has an ass like a horse."
"Ride it."
"Because her legs are like tree trunks. They crucify me."
"Be crucified. You always said you were a reincarnation of Jesus Christ."

Screw similes. Fuck metaphors. You can take your immortality, Alex, and stuff it. It's no longer my concern. Nor is my mortality your concern. Let the separation begin. *Your* poems, *my* life. Your compulsion to turn life into words is not mine. Not any longer.

———❖———

For hours I sit gazing out of the window at the snow, my hands circling the baby who is turning fluttery somersaults inside me. I'm thinking. Not fantasizing or daydreaming, but thinking. Thinking hard. And I'm deeply ashamed. I wasn't able to kill my mother in myself. I had to wait for Fanya to die and, in dying, to free me. But I'm going to forgive myself because I'm grateful to have done it any way at all. The crucial thing is that it's done. My mother died and now I'm free to be a woman. This frees me to be a daughter and a mother. Maybe that's what the wise baby was waiting for and why it has decided to stay.

Be glad, Alex, be glad that I don't have to wait for your literal death to be free of you. Now you can really begin to exist for me.

The circle closes.

I'm helping Alex pack his things. Clearing him out. Erasing his prints. There are empty spaces everywhere. The bookshelves look like mouths from which most of the teeth have been extracted. Drawers which were bursting with socks and underwear are empty. The Mother Hubbard wardrobe is bare, the hooks which held Alex's belts and scarves exposed — they look naked and forlorn. The bathroom is reduced to a state of asepsis. The empty space left in the toothbrush holder gapes. Somehow that's what hurts most — the absence of Alex's toothbrush. The mark of finality. Its absence makes me understand finally, absurdly, what his absence is going to mean. It's a burial process and I find myself waiting for the funeral procession to begin. But no rituals exist for the death of a marriage, as they do for the birth of one. Surely there should be a ceremony of divestment, a procession down the stairs and out the front door. A formal handing over of the keys, a dirge, a fanfare, the keening of friends and relatives; the drinking of champagne, cola, hemlock.

Something to mark the occurrence of an event as final and consequential as anything that happens in one's life.

The bags stand packed, the hand is proferred. Does one kiss? Hug? Cry? Smile? Scream? The door clicks shut. Each half of the whole stands on either side, hesitating. . . . We can hear each other breathing through the wooden partition.

Again I clamp my mouth shut. All I have to do is open it, let a sound come out — any sound — and Alex, who is standing on one side of the door, will miraculously materialize on the other. His scattered Startrek molecules will regroup themselves and we'll play the movie backwards. Socks will fly upstairs into drawers, suits will waltz back onto lonely hangers, scarves will clothe destitute hooks, and the toothbrush, with a soggy sigh of relief, will nestle into the domestic comfort of its porcelain hole.

It will take only one word for these miracles to occur. One word. But no. I clamp my hand over my mouth. No more words. Like a grey flavourless wad of overchewed gum, they hold the shape of too many people's mouths. . . .

The threatening emptiness has finally arrived. It's here. It's now. Only I can fill it.

I.

Me.

Myself.

I have to make a huge space between us — me, you. But the pain is enormous. Overwhelming. Separating myself from you is like reliving my mother's death — I'm twice orphaned. My heart is aching. Literally aching. I can see it lying in my chest. It looks like one of those shiny bright-red cartoon hearts with a jagged crack right down its centre.

To leave you, Alex, is to leave myself. To leave myself is to find myself. You are my childhood and now that you are severed from me I have to —

stop sucking my thumb
stop pulling the rags from my Aunty Milly's hollow chest
stop stomping on my father's silent feet
stop being afraid that my mother is going to let go of the
   windowsill
stop making caterpillars dance on hot meat.

I'm not even sure I'll be able to make it.

We're Siamese twins. Alexanna. Alexanna's Bad-time Band. Which twin has the liver? Which the heart? Will one survive? Will both? Or will the music stop forever when we're chopped off from each other?

The questions don't stop. My mind returns to them like a tongue to a decayed tooth.

Have I made my mother up? Did I cheat myself of a warm, loving mother? Have I made Alex up? Did I cheat myself of a warm, loving husband? Am I making myself up? Have I cheated myself of a warm, loving me?

Fact/fiction. Fiction/fact. Where does one begin and the other leave off?

Where does the truth lie? Or does the truth always lie?

Hard questions. Harder answers. Because there are no answers. It's time to stop digging for them. Time to pull my fingers out of the sticky honey pot of the past.

The only reality I can trust is the baby inside me. I don't want it to be trapped against a typewriter roll with forty-four deadly hammers bashing the life out of it. I want it to come leaping away from me, severing the umbilical cord as it flies. Biting through with its hard strong gums and spitting out the shreds.

I'm sorry I hurt you, Alex. I'm sorry I hurt me.

It's enough.

The hole is filled.

Stop shovelling, Srulik.

Stop shovelling.

Stop.

In order to become somebody's mother, I have to be nobody's daughter.